The FIGHT of your LIFE

WINNING IN LIFE BY FIRST WINNING IN YOUR MIND

Kenneth Estrada

The Fight of Your Life
Copyright © 2023 by Kenneth Estrada
All rights reserved.
ISBN: 979-8-39201-382-1
www.kennethestrada.com

To my wife, my best friend, my ministry partner.
Lynette, I love you more today than I ever have before in
my life. Tomorrow, I will love you more than I did today.
The day after... well, you get the point.

Thank you for being such an encouragement and
believing in me even in times when I didn't believe in
myself.
May you be rewarded greatly for the honor and love for
God and towards me as your husband that you continue
to model with such authenticity.

———————————————————

To my kids, I love our laughs, our teaching moments, and
having you all involved in some way in what God has
called me to do.
Thank you for the honor of being your dad.

ENDORSEMENTS

What a great book! Kenneth has taken a subject that is very important to our success in this life and thoroughly explained it. In *"The Fight of Your Life"*, you will learn how not only get rid of wrong thoughts, but how to build safe strongholds, which will be life changing for all of us. This book is full of practical examples from Kenneth and Lynette's life that will help your life. Thank you, Kenneth, for sharing this important message with the Body of Christ. You will enjoy this book, it blessed me, and I know it will bless and help you as well.

Mark Garver, Senior Pastor
Cornerstone Word of Life Church
Madison, Alabama

The Fight of Your Life is a timely book written for this generation. As a society we have seen mental health come under attack like never before. This book will train you how to win this battle and be victorious from the inside out. It's time for us to strengthen ourselves in God's word and this resource is the perfect mix of humor and personal examples to make Gods word come alive in our hearts.

Joel Sims, Lead Pastor
Word of Life Church
Jackson, Mississippi

In *The Fight of Your Life*, Kenneth Estrada reminds readers of their place in spiritual battle - We aren't fighting for victory, but from victory! He brazenly shares with us the necessary tools to effectively renew our minds on a consistent basis. He is candid about his highs and lows on his own faith journey from cover to cover. You will be blessed by his testimony and powerful teaching of God's faithfulness from start to finish.

Denise Hagin Burns, Executive Pastor
RHEMA Bible Church
Broken Arrow, Oklahoma

Many believers neglect the importance of the renewal of the mind, unaware of the fight required to overcome the past. However, this battle is real, and it is won by changing the way we speak and think. In this book, Kenneth Estrada gives the tools necessary to have the life God has ordained. I love the practicality he gives, to "stop going over old history over and over again" and to instead walk in our God-given authority. Any believer struggling with the past can take their rightful place and move forward by applying the truths in this book. Get ready to begin to live the way you were born to live.

DeWayne L. Wright, Lead Pastor
Kingdom Living Ministries
Perth Amboy, New Jersey

Pastor Kenneth Estrada is a dear friend of mine that I have known for over 10 years. He is a man of integrity and faith which are displayed in his book *"The*

Fight of Your Life". This book sums up how Kenneth lives his life and leads his church - absolute faith in God and His Word. What I appreciate the most in his writing is that he gives real life examples of how to deal with the storms and challenges of life from the position of our victory in Christ. He methodically shows you how to overcome by the Word of God being in your heart, your mind, your mouth, and your actions. I highly recommend to anyone, no matter where they are on their spiritual journey, to read and feed on this book, *"The Fight of Your Life"*.

Greg Squires, Lead Pastor
Freedom Life Church
Kissimmee, Florida

Kenneth is as authentic as they come! His down to earth illustrations and applications in *"The Fight of Your Life"* will give you the spiritual insight and practical know how to overcome and win every battle you face in your soul.

Aaron & Errin Hankins, Lead Pastors
Christian Worship Center
Alexandria, Louisiana

CONTENTS

Acknowledgments   xi

FOREWORD   1

INTRODUCTION   3

1   DEPRIVED OF POWER   13

2   THE NEED FOR RENEWED MINDS   25

3   ESCAPE THE LOOP   39

4   THE PROPER RESPONSE   65

5   SWAT IT DOWN   81

6   DON'T FEED THE STRAYS   99

7   THE POWER OF WORDS   111

8   WHO IS CONTROLLING YOUR SOUL?   119

9   THE UNCONTROLLED SOUL   133

10   BUILDING A SAFE STRONGHOLD   149

11   CONFESSIONS FOR A HEALTHY SOUL   163

ACKNOWLEDGMENTS

Many thanks to:

Our staff, for working so diligently week in and week out as I worked on the completion of this book. I can never pay you what you're worth because even if we could come to a number, I believe you are worth way more than that.

Our Kingdom Life family, for following my lead as I follow Christ. It continues to be an absolute honor to be called your pastor.

To my dad, for giving me the opportunity to be in ministry with you and trusting me with your vision.

To my mom, for taking some transcripts with a bunch of fillers and starting to get this book in motion though they were only a few pages.

To Julene Martin, for listening to all those messages and taking it upon yourself to transcribe them. Though it took years to complete, thank you for wanting this book to be released so badly so that others can be impacted by some of the same words you heard.

FOREWORD

"The Fight of Your Life" is a powerful and on-time book about how to use your faith in God to face impossible situations and to overcome them. Kenneth Estrada shares personal testimonies and practical instructions to demonstrate how you can win in the battlefield of your mind and emotions using the truth of God's Word. He says, "The quality of our lives is in direct proportion to the quality of our thoughts."

As you practice the teaching found in this book, you will experience victory and blessing in every area of life.

Dr. Mark Hankins
Mark Hankins Ministries

INTRODUCTION

It was Sunday morning, November 9th, 2008 and my wife Lynette was just a few days away from the birth of our beautiful little girl. My pregnant wife and I were the young pastors of a church we planted just a few years earlier. A few months prior to this particular Sunday, we had just relocated the church from the 2nd story of a shopping plaza in Orlando, FL to an elementary school in Poinciana, FL. While working harder than we ever had at that time, we were so excited about all that the future held for us as we followed God's plan for our lives.

I guess you could say that we were kind of "hard core" because even though we knew that our baby girl could arrive any day, Lynette still led worship that Sunday at church. If you've ever seen my wife worship, you know that she's extremely energetic, passionate, and gives her all! That Sunday, after the team was done leading us all in praise and worship, I got up to minister a word from God that I still, to this day, cannot tell you a word of what I preached or what it was even about, and it wasn't because I wasn't prepared or didn't have notes.

I was just a few minutes into my introduction of this message when my wife and a few ladies came out of the bathroom at the back of the auditorium of this elementary school. I noticed that they were not escorting my wife to her seat in the front row but rather they were leaving through one of the side exits at the back. To make matters worse, one of the young ladies accompanying my wife stood at the back trying to get my attention. She was motioning a "cut" sign at her throat with what seemed like her eyes popping out of their sockets and then walked out after the rest of them. Finally, someone came close to me to let me know that my wife's water broke but she wanted me to keep preaching while she was going home to wait for me. It was at this time that I had no idea what to do. I thought to myself, "'Do I wrap it up and say goodbye to everyone?', 'What exactly am I preaching on again?', 'Oh no, there's a first-time guest here and I can't believe that this is her first experience with us!'" When I felt like I'd spoken enough, I stopped talking and just hoped that at least one thing I said made sense. I immediately went to this guest to introduce myself and said, "I'm so sorry but I was so distracted because they came to tell me that my wife was about to have our baby". I then swallowed my pride and said, "PLEASE COME BACK!" I then rushed out the exit to the car to get home to my wife (something that I should've done immediately).

HERE COMES THE BABY...

Like a good husband, I arrived home to check on my wife and take her to the hospital. I was excited and nervous all at the same time as I pulled into the garage of the house we were living in at the time. When I walked into the house, to my surprise, I found my wife talking, laughing, and cooking. I thought, "What are you doing?! We should be on our way to the hospital!"

Lynette explained to me that she wasn't really feeling anything that felt like contractions, and she heard that we shouldn't go into the hospital too early because they could send us back home. After doing some research, however, we decided to load up the car and go on ahead to the hospital. After checking in, a nurse hooked up some kind of monitor to my wife to check her and the baby's vitals. While she was still talking with us, she said, "Whoa! You didn't feel that?!" My wife was having contractions and didn't even know it. This could be because she is secretly a superhero, and her pain tolerance is nowhere near that of us earthlings. They then started to suggest that she take certain medicines that would help to speed up the process.

HERE COMES THE CHALLENGE...

I'd like to remind you that we checked into the hospital early Sunday evening. Without going too far into details, I'm about to share a few things with you that we had to deal with. My intention is not to give place for anyone to get into fear but rather, to walk you through the beginning of a challenging moment that we walked through. The good news is that we came out on the other side victorious!

Although my wife's water had broken that unforgettable Sunday morning, our daughter decided that she was going to take her sweet time before coming into this world. Due to some of the medicine that they administered to Lynette, she began to feel the contractions come on stronger and it became more painful for her. We went from her having huge contractions that she didn't feel to now having these painful contractions that she definitely felt. This went on all the way through Monday with her making the decision to take the epidural because of how intense the pain got. Where was I this entire time, you ask? I was right there with her feeling every single contraction (after the epidural wore off) by her squeezing my hand as I stood by her side. I must pause to remind you that she had these superhuman powers and that I, being a mere earthling, was her loving husband. Her ability to take pain then transformed into an ability to dish out pain and I was on the receiving end. Because I thought I was going to pass out from the pain, (and she probably needed something firmer), I tried to give her something more solid that she could squeeze. She took it, tried it, then tossed it and said, with a strong voice that got really deep, *"No! GIVEEEE... MEEEE... YOURRRR... HAAAAAND!"*

We were now lacking sleep since we'd both been up since before church on Sunday morning. The early morning hours of Tuesday arrived and still no beautiful baby girl! It was 1:00 am and still, we were not quite there. Then 2:00 am... 3:00 am... 4:00

am and still nothing. I believe that by this time, Lynette started feeling sorry for me and told me to go lay down.

A CHALLENGE WE NEVER FACED...

At some point during the 4:00 AM hour, after I'd just closed my eyes for what was maybe 15-20 minutes, I woke up to my healthy wife having a seizure on the hospital bed. Now, I want you to understand that Lynette at that time was one of the healthiest individuals that I knew. She exercised regularly, ate healthily, and also took all-natural supplements and vitamins. She never had any kind of health issues in her entire life up until that point.

I ran to the door of the hospital room to call for help and then began praying with authority. Her OBGYN had just decided the night before that we were going to schedule a C-section at 5:00 AM that day and arrived when all of this started to happen. Thank God I knew how to pray and that I had some people that I could call as reinforcements. I called my mom and she then called her prayer group in St. Thomas. While all of this is happening, my mind is being bombarded with all kinds of thoughts. The devil is showing me pictures of losing both my wife and my baby. He then sends thoughts and pictures of me having to raise this baby by myself. I start wondering, *"Will I ever marry again?"* I'm thinking, *"I probably need to get married again because I can't raise and take care of this girl all by myself."* All of these thoughts come in a matter of seconds!

They invite me into the operating room and there lies Lynette. She's conscious, but I can see the look of worry and despair on her face. The anesthesiologist administers a certain kind of medicine through her IV before they began to operate. Lynette then looks at me and says, *"Babe, I can feel it coming on me again..."* She then has another seizure right there on the operating table. My wife, who has never had any complications, all of a sudden is looking completely different and has now had two seizures within an hour. Once again, I take my place of authority and she comes back to normal. Finally, they conduct the C-section and deliver our sweet baby Kezia during the 5:00 AM hour on Tuesday, November 11th.

I wish that I could tell you that this was the hardest battle that we had to fight but I can't. What took place after these events was a more tiresome and challenging battle than what we dealt with during those three days. I've worded this true account with transparency while using humor because I believe that what I'm going to be sharing in this book will help those that read it.

You may never go through something like we did, or you may be currently dealing with a situation that's way more intense than what we dealt with, but with the information that you will read about in this book, you can be helped. I don't want you to just read it and receive some "information" but rather, I want you to ask the Holy Spirit to give you "revelation" as you study along with me in this book. Jesus' victory is our victory and we can walk in the victory He provided for us. God told us in His word that we ought to fight the good fight of faith *(1 Timothy 6:12)*. If we are going to do that effectively, we will need to be on guard against Satan's strategy of trying to hold us in the mental arena which is his main battleground. Our greatest battles will be held in the mental arena so you can say that this is the Fight of Your Life. My prayer for you is that with the help of this book, you will be strengthened in your spirit to keep him in the arena of faith by responding to wrong thoughts with the Word of God coming right up out of your spirit.

CHAPTER ONE
DEPRIVED OF POWER

Have you ever felt powerless? If your answer is yes, you're not alone. Oftentimes, when people go through tough and challenging times, they feel powerless also. As believers, it is imperative that we understand that we are actually not without power in a difficult situation. In fact, we have actually been given power over our enemy who is the one who initiates many of these challenges.

John 16:33 AMPC
"I have told you these things, so that in Me you may have [perfect] peace and confidence. In the world you have tribulation and trials and distress and frustration; but be of good cheer [take courage; be confident, certain, undaunted]! For I have overcome the world. [I have deprived it of power to harm you and have conquered it for you.]"

During those days leading up to the birth of our daughter Kezia, which I wrote about in the introduction of this book, it would've been easy for me to feel powerless as a husband and soon-to-be father. Unfortunately, that was not the end of the challenge because the battle we faced afterward was far greater. I'm happy to report to you that Lynette had no more seizures and recovered well in her body. The fight that we did have to fight, however, was the fight in her soul — really it was a fight in both of our thought lives.

You see, my wife, when she was younger, struggled with fear for a period of time in her life. After going through what she did during the birth of

Kezia, here comes this big battle that would seem like there was no way out for us. My wife was constantly being tormented with thoughts of death, fear of having another seizure, and any other evil thing her mind could think up.

There were multiple trips to the Emergency Room and all kinds of tests that she wanted to do because she "felt" like there was something wrong with her. While this was happening with her, here I am trying to be supportive while dealing with thoughts myself. She was not the Lynette that I married and I wondered if I would ever get my wife back.

I can remember feeling concerned about her mental state. Once again, the thoughts of whether or not I was going to have to raise this baby by myself were coming back to me. She wasn't bonding with our newborn baby which was so unlike her nature. Some situations got better as the weeks went on but there were other areas that took months and even years. This was an attack straight from the enemy and we needed to fight. We needed to fight the good fight of faith!

1 Timothy 6:12 AMPC
12 Fight the good fight of the faith; lay hold of the eternal life to which you were summoned and [for which] you confessed the good confession [of faith] before many witnesses.

NOT FOR…. FROM!

While faith is referred to in the verse mentioned earlier (1 Timothy 6:12) as a good fight, we are not just talking about the fight **of** faith but also the fight **to** faith. The great news is, God calls it a good fight! A good fight is one that you win. Now we understand this, that we are not fighting **for** victory, but we are fighting **from** the standpoint of victory. In other words, we are victorious. So, we are not trying to get God to give us something. It already belongs to us.

Let me try to illustrate it to you this way in my attempt to bring clarification. Have you ever played the game "King of the Hill"? It's a game that some of us played as kids. The objective was to get to the top of an agreed upon hill (in a playground setting) and maintain that position. If your team made it up the hill first, you fought with all of your might to hold that position. You were actually at an advantage if you made it to the top first because others trying to "take the hill" were still climbing and exerting energy, hoping to get you out of position and back down to the bottom. If you were at the top, you would still use energy to fight off the other opponents in order to defend your position. However, it was easier because you were at a "position of rest" rather than a "climbing position". You could use your weight to push down your enemy and watch them roll down the hill. You were not still trying to take the hill "fighting" FOR victory. Because you were already at the top, you were "fighting" FROM that position of victory. All you had to do was maintain and hold that position.

*...we are not fighting **for** victory, but we are fighting **from** a standpoint of victory.*

Jesus Christ, through His death, burial, and resurrection has already fought the ultimate battle and WON the victory for us. That means that Satan is already defeated and has been conquered. Sometimes, through our actions, we act like our "fight" is us trying to accomplish something that maybe Jesus forgot to do. We are now "In Christ" and His victory was won for us and we have equal victory with him. We have been positioned in Christ — in a place of victory! Hold that position and fight the good fight of faith from there!

THE FIGHT CONTINUES...

Lynette and I had a battle on our hands that we weren't anticipating that we would have to fight. Here we were leading a church, preaching faith, "grabbing a cornstalk, swinging out over hell and spitting in the devil's eye" (like Pastor Mark Hankins would say), and praying for people in the middle of all their mess. While we were in the middle of God's will, these attacks arrived at our doorstep.

Jesus Christ, through His death, burial, and resurrection has already fought the ultimate battle and WON the victory for us.

There were many nights of Lynette waking up in the middle of the night in a state of panic. Fear would grip her so severely that she would feel as though she couldn't even function properly. All kinds of false symptoms that appeared to be real would grip her and make her think that something was wrong with her and that she was going to die. I would have to be up with her doing my best to help get her thinking in line with the Word of God.

I think many believers somehow have the misconception that walking by faith means that they should be able to follow God's plan for their lives with no challenges or struggles along the way.

Rick Renner, a wonderful Greek scholar of New Testament Greek words, stated that the word "fight" is the Greek word *agonidzo*. He described it as referring to a struggle, a fight, great exertion, or effort. It is actually where we get the word agony — a word that was often used in the New Testament to convey the ideas of anguish, pain, distress, and conflict. He also said that "the word *agonidzo* itself comes from the word *agon*, which is the word that depicted the athletic conflicts and competitions that were so famous in the ancient world. It frequently pictured wrestlers in a wrestling match, with each wrestler struggling with all his might to overcome his opponent in an effort to hurl him to the ground in a fight to the finish".

...many believers somehow have the misconception that walking by faith means that they should be able to follow God's plan for their lives with no challenges or struggles along the way.

YOU ARE AN OVERCOMER

There is a fight to faith, and it involves the fight of your life. However, this fight does not necessarily take place the way that many think that it does. The Bible tells us that we are an overcomer in Christ Jesus. That indicates then that there are still certain things that we must overcome, otherwise we cannot be considered an overcomer.

21

There are challenges, we understand this. There are pressures of life. Jesus even said that as long we are in this world there will be temptations, there will be trials, there will be tribulations, there will be pressures. But He says, *"be of good cheer for I have overcome the world"*. The Amplified Bible goes on to say, *"and I have deprived it of its power to harm you"*.

God wants us to know that in middle of the trials, in the middle of the tribulations, we can go ahead and get happy. We can go ahead and be joyful. We can, as James says, *"count it all joy,"* when we fall into various trials and various temptations (James 1:2). There is nothing you can do to escape these trials. Death may seem to offer a way of escape, but you should not want to go before your time, and you do not have to go until you are satisfied.

This is also relevant to the fight of your life because sometimes people say, *"Well, it was just their time to go"*. What are you talking about?! They were 16 years old! The Bible says, *"with long life, I will satisfy you"*. If I get to the age of 90 and I'm still not satisfied with life, then I'm not planning on going anywhere. That promise from God means I can live a long life. I can live a healthy life. I can live a prosperous life. You don't have to walk around with a "long face" just because you're 90. You can just enjoy life! You can enjoy life in your teen years. You can enjoy life in your 20's and your 30's and your 40's and your 50's. You can even be happy in your 90's. You can just be getting started despite your age.

Smith Wigglesworth, a great man of faith from the early 1900's, didn't get started in the ministry until he was 50. Your age need not be a deterrent to embracing God's plan for your life. Sometimes, when people hear the word ministry, they immediately think of pulpit ministry. But ministry simply means service in whatever capacity God has called you to serve. It may be "workplace" ministry. God has anointed you for where you are, to do whatever it is He has called you to do during that season of life. God can open doors for you that cause you to be a blessing to the Body of Christ. I believe that there are some believers that need to work in government so that they can open some doors for the Body of Christ to help advance the kingdom of God. Go there and open some doors for the gospel to go out. There are some individuals that are called to the medical field. Who knows whether or not while you are there with a dying patient, you could lay hands on that person and command life into their body and the patient recovers as a testimony to the power of God and the authority of the believer?

Know that there is an anointing upon your life to do whatever it is that God has called you to do. But there are certain things and certain challenges that you and I are going to have to overcome. There is a fight to faith. But it is a good fight because God has already deprived the world of its power to harm you.

CHAPTER TWO

THE NEED FOR RENEWED MINDS

I grew up as a PK (pastor's kid) and I would sit in church just about every service. It's a practice that now that I'm older and wiser, I'm so appreciative that my parents raised us that way. Though I may not have paid attention every single time that my dad or another minister was speaking, I believed that what was being taught was great. My dad would deliver a message that challenged us yet brought such hope to those that listened to the word being taught. However, if I can be honest with you, there was something that would often bother me.

I would look at the lives of the wonderful people that were coming to our church and notice that there were some that were living proof of God's goodness. At the same time, there were others who were saying "amen" in response to the preaching, but it seemed like God wasn't noticing their struggles.

I would wonder, *"why does it seem like this person over here is living such a good life but here is this other person who heard the same messages but looking at their life, you couldn't tell that God was good to them?"* It just didn't seem fair to me! They genuinely loved God and believed that He was good. They were sincere but why did it seem like it wasn't working for them?

...the quality of our lives are in direct proportion to the quality of our thoughts.

What I've come to realize, as I continue to grow in revelation of God's word, is that it was never God's fault that they weren't receiving His best. As a matter of fact, He has already blessed us with every spiritual blessing in the heavenly places in Christ Jesus (Ephesians 1:3).

We don't have to talk God into being good to us. He always wants to be good to His kids! But we do have a part to play in our receiving from Him.

Do you remember what happened when Jesus went to His hometown (Mark 6:1-6) and couldn't do any mighty work there? He marveled at their unbelief, but He didn't leave them there! He didn't leave them without a "cure" for the unbelief that hindered them.

Mark 6:6 NKJV
"And He marveled because of their unbelief. Then He went about the villages in a circuit, teaching."

Jesus knew that, though He was the Son of God and anointed to heal the sick, He would be limited by what He could do there because of their inability to receive the life that He possessed. What was His solution then? He went around the villages teaching! He was working on their ability to receive from God. It's not as if Jesus was lacking power or just had a bad day. Their unbelief hindered them from receiving from God Himself, though they had Him in the flesh! Jesus knew that they needed their minds renewed so He purposed to teach them principles of the kingdom.

IMPROVE YOUR LIFE

When you think about it, the quality of our lives are in direct proportion to the quality of our thoughts. If you're not thinking right, then you won't be speaking right. In other words, our lives will equal our thought lives. It will reflect the thoughts that we dwell on the most — good or bad. If we want to improve our lives, we must make it a priority to improve our system of thinking. Wouldn't it be unfair if God just placed us here on this earth and didn't give us the means to do just that? The means that He gave us is through the renewing of our minds with the Word of God. This is not a one-time occurrence nor is it something that someone else can do for you. As important as prayer is, prayer alone will not solve your problem.

Deep inside every human being is a common character trait that plagues and affects us all. It is in the nature of our flesh to have a natural inclination to follow the path of least resistance. As a result of this, it is so easy to be lazy and that filters down into other areas of our lives. We want our pastor to get it for us. We're basically wanting them, and others, to live our spiritual lives for us because we don't want to be responsible. We start calling other ministries to pray for us. Some even post on their social media pages asking for prayer. Please don't misunderstand me, I'm not saying that we can't ask for prayer or receive counsel. What I am saying is that so many challenges can be turned into success if we would become more diligent and improve our thinking.

The responsibility falls on us and not with God to renew our minds. We must take the Word of God, which has the power to transform our minds, and spend time renewing our minds with it. This will discipline our minds to think in line with His Word.

The responsibility falls on us and not with God to renew our minds.

When Lynette and I were in our battle with those wrong thoughts that were coming from the enemy, we had to discipline ourselves to take on the thoughts of God in His Word. No matter how trying your situation may seem, God has a way out for you and a place of peace that you can walk in that surpasses understanding. You can walk in perfect peace!

Romans 12:2 NKJV
"And do not be conformed to this world, but be transformed by the renewing of your mind, that you may prove what is that good and acceptable and perfect will of God."

God tells us that when we renew our mind with His word, it has the power to transform, and will transform our lives. You can say that your life won't even look the same! You won't be the same because of the power of God at work in you through that renewed mind. The people that are renewing their minds with the Word of God will accomplish things that they were unable to do before because of that transformation. That is how powerful a renewed mind is!

YOU "GOTTA" DO SOMETHING

Before we go further, I don't want to assume that everyone understands the true nature in which God created us. If you already know what I'm going to share then it will only strengthen what you already know. According to the Word of God, you are a three-fold being. Through revelation of the Word, we see that "man" is a spirit, he possesses a soul (consisting of our mind, our will, and our emotions), and he lives in a body. When you became a new creation in Christ through your confession of faith in Him, God immediately did something with your spirit. Your spirit was translated out of the kingdom of darkness and into the kingdom of light! He took that old raggedy spirit that had the nature of death and made you alive in Christ with a new spirit. That new spirit now has the life and nature of

32

God Himself in it! Although that happened, you still have the same mind and body that you did before you were born again. If you had "crusty" toes before you got saved, I'm sorry to inform you but you still have those same "crusty" toes. The Word shows us that we have to do something with our minds and with our bodies.

No matter how long you have been bound, your flesh doesn't have to run your life!

In Romans 12:1, the apostle Paul tells us that we have to do something with our bodies.

Romans 12:1 NKJV
"I beseech you therefore, brethren, by the mercies of God, that you present your bodies a living sacrifice, holy, acceptable to God, which is your reasonable service."

Paul states that *you*, the real "you"— your spirit, must present *your* body to God for His glory.

We can see throughout the New Testament that he accomplished so much for God's glory. How was he able to do so? He kept his body under subjection. He did that so he could avoid being disqualified (1 Corinthians 9:27). He brought his body into subjection to his born again, recreated human spirit. He, his spirit, dominated and ruled — not his body. Although you are saved, your body is still going to want to do wrong. That's the reason why we must develop our spirits and, as we are strengthened through time in the Word and prayer, we will keep our flesh in check. No matter how long you have been bound, your flesh doesn't have to run your life!

NOT JUST YOUR BODY...

It would be one thing if all we had to deal with was our body but it's just not so. We have to do something with our minds. We must renew our minds because whoever controls the soul dictates the destiny of our lives. If your flesh is in charge of your soul (mind), your flesh will determine your quality of life. You just can't leave it up to your flesh. God's way is so much better! When you renew your mind, you start thinking differently. You may have thought one way, but after renewing your mind you realize, *"I'm seeing this differently than I did before... I can't think the same way about this as I used to"*. You actually replace the old way you thought with how God thinks. You start making His thoughts your own!

We must renew our minds because whoever controls the soul dictates the destiny of your life. If your flesh is in charge of your soul (mind), your flesh will determine your quality of life. You just can't leave it up to your flesh. God's way is so much better!

God's thoughts, which we find from His

Word, so often go against natural human reasoning. The more you feed on God's Word the easier it becomes to act on it. A perfect picture of a renewed mind is one that consumes the Word of God and then acts on it. If your thinking is in opposition to what the Word of God says, lay those thoughts aside and instead take on the thoughts found in the Word.

For the person who has an unrenewed mind, that individual will struggle and even argue with the Word. That unrenewed mind will try to reason but a mind that is renewed with the Word will come into agreement with what God has said in His Word. There are a lot of followers of Christ that wish they were spiritual giants, but they aren't willing to do what is necessary to renew their minds. If only they realized how powerful they are when their spirit and their mind come into agreement. We can renew our minds to a place where our automatic response in the face of opposition is to think thoughts of faith and then act in faith.

KEEP THE STINK OUT

This will not be an overnight process, but it is one that you're going to have to keep at every day of your life. Fight the urge to stay on the path of least resistance. You can bring your thoughts in line with God's. My wife has said for years, *"Your mind will stay renewed just as much as your teeth stay brushed"*. Trust me, your friends will be happy that you maintain a practice of brushing your teeth daily. If you don't, you may not die but you will have a "stink mouth". It's the same with renewing your mind. If you don't do it, you may not necessarily die but you will be walking around with "stink thoughts". To me that is worse than a "stink mouth".

A perfect picture of a renewed mind is one that consumes the Word of God and then acts on it.

In other words, just as it is necessary to brush your teeth daily, you need to have the same practice with the Word of God.

We can keep the stink out as we renew our mind with God's Word. You replace the stink — you exchange the wrong thoughts with the right ones as you do. Why? Simply because:

- If your thinking stinks, then your believing will stink.
- If your believing stinks, then your speaking will stink.
- If your speaking stinks, then your actions will stink.
- And then if your actions stink, your whole life is gonna stink!

Can you see how wrong thinking opens the door to the devil? Don't give the devil any place in your life! Renewing your mind will be one of your greatest defenses against the enemy in this fight of your life.

CHAPTER THREE

ESCAPE THE LOOP

Technology has been changing at a rapid pace. I'm from the generation that listened to music on vinyl records, cassette tapes, and CDs. Growing up, we weren't allowed to listen, much less purchase, "secular" music. I remember as a teen listening to the radio trying to record my favorite songs on blank cassette tapes and doing my best to stop the recording before the radio station announces their call sign. Some people won't understand what it was like for us to go from that to CDs and then digital downloads. We went from storing vinyl records, cassettes, and CDs in towers, albums, and boxes to the ability to carry thousands of songs on a small handheld device that we also use as a phone.

Some of you may remember how annoying it was for a CD that you were listening to be scratched. Your favorite song would start skipping and soon something that you loved to hear is now an annoyance. What happens many times with a lot of us as believers is that we operate almost like a scratched CD that skips and plays the same thing over and over again.

Some years ago, I was watching a show on a television channel, and for some reason, every time it came to the end of a commercial break, the show would repeat the scene I had just watched. But I had seen that already, and I wanted to get to the next scene. I wanted to see what was next. But there was a glitch that was causing a loop to take place.

...thoughts of doubt may come but we do not have to entertain them

We do the same thing where we throw a loop and play wrong thoughts over and over in our minds. What then happens is the more we think on those things, they eventually get into our hearts. Remember, as we discussed earlier in this book, when the scripture says, "*and entertain no inner doubt,*" it infers that thoughts of doubt may come but we do not have to entertain them. You can say, "*I resist doubt*". Fear will try to come but you can say, "*No, no, no, fear, I don't accept you. I resist fear, I'm strong in the Lord and in the power of His might.*" "*God has not given me the spirit of fear, but of power, love and a sound, disciplined mind.*" That's what a sound mind means. A sound mind is a disciplined mind. Now that's something good to say, because your mind is your own. You can have control of your thought life. After all, they are your thoughts — you can control them.

"...IT'S YOUR DREAM!"

Now everybody can't do what I'm about to say. But in the past, I used to have nightmares a lot as a kid. I didn't like nightmares and I used to fear them and not want to go back to sleep. But when I started getting more serious about the things of God and understanding my authority, whenever I had a bad dream, I'd say, *"Devil you are such a liar. I'm going back and I'm going to dream that dream again and change it, it's my dream!"*

I remember hearing a funny story about a lady who dreamt that this large monster was chasing her until she got backed into a corner and she said, *"Oh my God, oh my God, what are you going to do, what are you going to do?!"* In her dream, the monster said, *"I don't know! It's your dream!"* And the truth of the matter is, it is. It's the same with your thoughts, they are yours and you

42

have control over them. You're the one that has the authority to cast that thought down. If it is contrary to the word of God, if it is contrary to the will of God, if it is contrary to what you're believing God for according to God's word, you can say "no" to it. You can say *"I believe I am who God says I am, I have what God says I have, I can do what God says I can do."*

BOUNCE IT!

I can recall years ago hearing Keith Moore teaching along these lines. He said someone came up to him, and said, *"Brother Keith, I get it now, it's like, you've got to have a bouncer outside your mind."* Those employed as bouncers at a club have the authority to say who can and cannot enter the club. If it's an invitation-only event, you do not get past the bouncer without your name being on the list or showing your invitation. Therefore, when that thought comes knocking on the door of your mind, you've got to put that "bouncer" outside of your mind and not allow certain things to come in. Picture this scenario:

Bouncer: "Who are you?"
Wrong thought: "I'm a thought of fear."
Bouncer: "Ah no, you ain't welcome in here."

Bouncer: "Who are you?"
Wrong thought: "Well, you know, right now I'm really concerned about the money."
Bouncer: "No, you ain't allowed in here."

Bam! Shut the door! Close it! Bounce that thought out!

It has to be like that. You can't allow any thought that's not on the list, God's will for your life, to enter your heart. If you believe that you have no control over your thought life, then you are in trouble! You do have authority over your thought life in whichever area you are being tormented.

VAIN THOUGHTS

Whenever our behavior digresses from the way God has mandated in His Word how we should be in His kingdom, we need to look at the reason why.

You can't allow any thought that's not on the list, God's will for your life, to enter your heart.

The Bible refers to vain thoughts, which is what gives birth to that deviated behavior.

Psalm 119:113 KJV
"I hate vain thoughts: but thy law do I love."

In the context of the verse, vain is described in the dictionary as empty, useless, worthless, devoid of meaning, or scripturally put, not profitable or with no purpose. Anything that doesn't align with the principles of God or can't be found in the Bible is vain. In short, thoughts that do not produce anything of value are vain. Vain thoughts, or we can use the term vain imaginations, will paint a portrait of our lives on the basis of anything outside of God's plan for us found in His Word.

The LORD is addressing how we think. The Psalmist was making it very clear that loving (enjoying) vain thoughts and loving the law of God (the Word of God) cannot co-exist in someone's life. We cannot serve two masters. Either we will hate vain thoughts and love the Word of God, or we will do the opposite. We cannot be double-minded. This was actually made clear if we read a few verses earlier.

Psalms 119:103-104 NKJV
"How sweet are <u>Your words</u> to my taste, Sweeter than honey to my mouth! <u>Through Your precepts I get understanding; Therefore I hate every false way.</u>"

When you look at the word "therefore", this demonstrates to us that we can't afford to have a co-existence in our minds of thinking on things that are false (contrary to God's Word), and a love for the Word of God (which is truth). Our ability to swat down and eliminate vain thoughts and instead correctly focus our thought life is critical to this fight of faith. Although Lynette and I have had challenges come against us over the years, this was key for us to walk and continue in the victory that Jesus provided for us.

WHO CONTROLS YOUR CULTURE?

I taught a series of teaching at our church called *"The Battle for Culture"*. In that series, I explain how every kingdom has a culture. The invisible realm consists of the kingdom of light and the kingdom of darkness. Colossians 1:13-14 says, *"He has delivered us from the power of darkness and conveyed us into the kingdom of the Son of His love, in whom we have redemption through His blood, the forgiveness of sins.*" Thank God we have been delivered and brought into the kingdom of the Son of His love! While that is true, we must understand that we still have an adversary. One important truth we need to realize is that whoever controls your thinking controls your culture — they control your way of life. Satan is always going to try to get you to side in with his way of thinking because he wants you to conform to the culture of his kingdom. He wants to control your culture. Here's a good reminder, we have weapons that are mighty in God!

2 Corinthians 10:3-5 KJV
"For though we walk in the flesh, we do not war after the flesh: (For the weapons of our warfare are not carnal, but mighty through God to the pulling down of strong holds;) Casting down imaginations, and every high thing that exalteth itself against the knowledge of God, and bringing into captivity every thought to the obedience of Christ;"

This is a fight that we ought not to back down from. The warfare for the control of your soul is described here in 2 Corinthians 10:3-5 and the battleground is found in your mind. On this battleground, you can find three levels of activity. The three levels we are going to discuss a little are:

1. THOUGHTS
2. IMAGINATIONS
3. STRONGHOLDS

LEVEL ONE: Thoughts

It's been said that over 6,000 thoughts come to the average person on a daily basis. They come from every direction and are transmitted to your brain through the things that you see, every word that you hear, and every encounter you have throughout your day.

You have the responsibility of choosing the thoughts that you dwell on. It's obvious that not all thoughts are good thoughts and that's why we have to recognize and learn to select the proper ones and cast down the wrong ones, that is, if you're gonna follow the culture of God's kingdom.

Wherever you find ignorance of God's Word you will find wrong thinking which produces wrong believing. That is why the devil thrives on ignorance. He needs that open door that comes from wrong believing, so he depends on ignorance for his plan to work. Thinking in line with the Word of God will keep the door shut to the enemy.

Wherever you find ignorance of God's word you will find wrong thinking which produces wrong believing.

The Word of God is the remedy that cures wrong thinking and believing. People often think wrong because of the signals they received from the culture of the kingdom they used to be a part of, the kingdom of darkness. When you get born-again, you must now have your mind renewed to how we think in the kingdom of God.

If you were never taught the Word of God or you sat under incorrect teaching, it will affect the way that you think. Another hindrance is formulating your own ideas about God and His actions. We need to discipline our minds to only accept that which is in line with the Bible — the constitution of God's kingdom.

In Matthew 6:25, we see clearly that Jesus told us to *"take no thought"* about even the things we need. That means then that we have the choice of what thoughts we're going to dwell on and allow to stay. The devil cannot make you take that thought. Not even God can force you to take the thoughts He wants you to take. The choice is ours! I don't know about you but I'm endeavoring to be better at doing my part to "take no thought".

LEVEL TWO: Imaginations

Your mind works by mental imagery. What that means is that we actually don't think in words but we think in images. For example, if by me attempting to describe something to someone who has their sight, I said, "Look over there at that blue truck," they are not picturing the words which are made up of the letters b-l-u-e t-r-u-c-k. Instead, in their mind they would see a mental image of a blue truck. That's how our mind functions as it receives signals. We need to understand how powerful this is for us. In Proverbs 23:7, we are told that as a man thinks in his heart, so is he. This truth is basically

We need to discipline our mind to only accept that which is in line with the Bible — the constitution of God's kingdom.

informing us that the quality of our life is directly related to how we think regularly.

When we meditate (ponder over and over) and think about a thought, we isolate that thought in the realm of our mind. We begin to paint a mental image in our imagination which eventually will produce behavior, our automatic response. So much of our patterns of response can be traced back to our programming in the earlier years of our lives. Through the different situations that come to us, we develop a mental conditioning, but all consistent behavior is rooted deep in our imagination. It's been said that the people that influenced you the most in the first 20 years of your life have played a major role in your mental conditioning. This may be discouraging to some who feel like they have been scarred because of certain environments they were exposed to growing up but there is still hope.

God designed and created your mind with the ability to bring His life found in Christ and have it manifested in our natural lives. Jesus told us that

He came so that we might have and experience life as God has it and enjoy it in abundance. In the kingdom of God, this is available to its citizens and the only way we become citizens is by being born-again. We are *born* citizens!

If you were to read the account of the people building the Tower of Babel in Genesis chapter 11, you can just see how powerful the imagination is. It was said in verse 6 that they all spoke the same language and that they were unified, but it also said that "nothing that they imagined to do" could be stopped. They kept a mental picture in their mind and had the Lord not scattered them, they would've accomplished their goal.

Psalm 2:1 KJV
"Why do the heathen rage, and the people imagine a vain thing?"

Psalm 2:1 AMPC
"WHY DO the nations assemble with commotion [uproar and confusion of voices], and why do the people imagine (meditate upon and devise) an empty scheme?"

The imagination can work for us but it can also work against us if we are not holding onto the right image. We can easily see that if you are using your imagination the wrong way, wrong behavior will be the byproduct. Don't meditate upon and devise empty schemes; useless, worthless, and purposeless mental imagery. Thoughts can be found at the very root of the matter when we look at our responses in behavior.

LEVEL THREE: Strongholds

Thoughts that are meditated on become imaginations as we gather mental pictures of those thoughts. Imaginations then become strongholds when the produced behavior is now something that consistently goes against your best interests. Strongholds come from wrong imaginations and reasonings that are contrary to the Word of God. You can locate the presence of a stronghold in your mind by recognizing besetting behaviors that are bad habits and even addictive and obsessive (compulsive). These wrong behaviors have actually been produced by wrong thoughts.

Every negative stronghold definitely must be dealt with. I think we need to remember that Satan is not all-knowing nor can he or any of his demons read our minds. What they do is listen to get their cues from our words. Those words reveal to them our vain thoughts. They also observe our lives to see our behaviors that go against the Word of God. When they receive those cues from us, they then go on the attack to attempt to bring us to this level of a stronghold. Circumstances in our lives become manipulated by them to add pressure, temptation, opportunities for offense, and the list could go on. This causes us to have multiple opportunities to continue in the wrong behavior.

Let me explain it to you by telling of one encounter I had with someone who wanted to break an addiction he had to a particular substance. He desired to do better and to no longer be bound and we were attempting to get him the help he needed. He made a statement that I found to be interesting. He said, *"It's like wherever I go it follows me. I don't even go looking for it."* He changed schools and went to an environment where no one knew him, yet he was approached with many opportunities to continue with substance abuse. You think that was a coincidence? No! His words and actions prior to that were observed by the kingdom of darkness.

I personally didn't have that challenge. Early in my teen years, I was presented with the opportunity to do drugs but because I said no each time, I haven't had multiple opportunities to partake in such a destructive habit. It was drilled in us as kids that drugs were bad, so I knew I didn't want to do it, especially since in my pre-teen years I was pressured to smoke toilet paper as a joke. That sucker will burn your chest! Don't ask me how I know... kids can be really dumb when they get around their friends.

I can't express enough how thankful I am that we have weapons to win this fight! It was written that they are mighty in God for the pulling down of strongholds! A stronghold is the first arena you have to deal with when it comes to casting down thoughts and dealing with vain imaginations. There is an anointing from God available to break that stronghold — that bondage over your life!

My reason for referring to it as a "negative stronghold" earlier is because we can actually build positive ones.

There is an anointing from God available to break that stronghold — that bondage over your life!

A stronghold is defined as:

1) *A fortified place or fortress*

2) *A place having strong defenses*

3) *A place of security*

We can actually build a strong, safe, and proper stronghold in our minds by thinking the right thoughts and getting them into our imagination. This is the position you want to get to because there is safety there. A little later in this book, I'd like to help you understand how this can be done.

Concerning negative strongholds, if you're married and you have started having thoughts concerning your spouse that are not good and are contrary to the will of God, if you allow that thought to come in and allow it to fester in your imagination, it's going to end up being a stronghold. That uncontrolled thought creates a vision and then that vision becomes a plan and then that plan gets executed.

There are some people who are on a repeat, on a loop, *"Oh well, you know, you don't understand what's going on in my life, it's hard, it's hard, it's hard.*" Sometimes they'll try to change it up a little bit if they realize they've been saying the same thing. But they are still on that loop, that repeat. Do you remember those turntables on which we played those vinyl records? The turntable was a major component of a record player. Some of my younger readers may need to do a web search on this. But a record player worked with a needle, so that, as the record rotated, music would play. But occasionally the needle would go into a groove and because the record was scratched, it would keep repeating the same refrain over and over again, until you physically moved the needle to a new position on the record, past that scratch.

Well, in the same way, examine what you've been talking about frequently because of the thoughts you've allowed to come in. I'm not saying that the trials and tribulations aren't there. But the Bible says that they are temporary, and everything that is temporary, everything that is seen, is subject to change. That's why He says focus on the things which are unseen because these things that are seen are temporary. They are subject to change.

The more you work on this the more it "irks" and agitates you when you hear people talking a certain way and saying the same thing. The word of God has the solution for any challenge or situation. The word of God has the thoughts of God because words are the containers of thoughts. Therefore, God's thoughts have the power to transform us. But I've found out that when we're in a challenge, rather than seeking the solution from God's word, we seek for sympathy from others. We want someone to "hear us out". But even though that's what we want, it's not always what we need. We need friends in

...examine what you've been talking about frequently because of the thoughts you've allowed to come in.

our lives who will let us know that we're on a loop. I'm thankful for friends that I have that make me aware when certain thoughts slip through that I didn't quite capture. It could have been a thought of doubt or thought of lack that showed up in my speech because words are containers of thoughts. So, what I needed at that time was not a sympathizer, but someone who would challenge me with "what does the word of God say concerning this subject?"

Every thought has the power to transform your life. The question is, what thoughts are you allowing to get in? I mean, is your bouncer not doing his job? Is he accepting bribes? Is he just letting anybody in because he's asleep on the job? Or is he a good bouncer, doing his job, and keeping out any unwelcome thoughts. This is the fight of your life. The fight of your life is with your thought life. And you can learn to master it.

Please hear me. You must capture those thoughts and swat them down. Don't say, *"You know, I'll let this thought stay here."* No, let that thought go. And really you can hit it so hard that it doesn't come back again. It's a fight, but there's a fight to faith, isn't there?

Every thought has the power to transform your life. The question is, what thoughts are you allowing to get in?

I used to have challenges with certain thoughts but now I'm not even affected by them anymore because, by the grace of God, I swatted them so hard that they haven't returned. I've swatted them down so hard that now the enemy and his little imps realize, *"Oh we've tried that thought before, we can't bring that to him again.*

Let's go back to the drawing board. Let's see if can get some different thoughts, because that thought, that one that we tried, was defective, it didn't work. I mean, he just swatted the mess out of that thought that it just didn't faze him at all." Don't let the enemy think he's winning! It's your mind! You can swat it so hard that the enemy won't try to bring it back again. This is the fight of your life.

There was a song in the '80s, 'Love is a Battlefield' but it's your mind that is a battlefield. It is a battlefield because of all the thoughts that bombard your mind. But you have been given authority by God and can defeat those thoughts and take them prisoner.

CHAPTER FOUR
THE PROPER RESPONSE

As a child growing up in the Caribbean, our culture placed a high importance on how we responded when we were spoken to. I can recall attending school in my pre-school and elementary years and being extremely shy. Because I was so shy, I had a very difficult time looking into someone's eyes when they were talking to me (a habit that continued into my years growing up) and my response to them wasn't any better. For some reason, many times I lacked the boldness to give a satisfactory response to some adults. There were multiple times when a teacher spoke to me or asked me a question and my response to them was a shaking or nodding of the head. I would then be told, *"That's not a proper response... use your words."* Actually, what was said to me a few times (in a Caribbean accent) was, *"You're not a dummy! Don't shake your head for me! Use your words!"*

I believe that what they were trying to instill in me was confidence. They were attempting to help me gain the ability to hold my head high and respond the way someone of status would. Even at home and at church, if I walked into a room where there were adults, it was expected that I used proper manners and greet the room with a "good morning, good afternoon, or good evening". As I think about it now, because I was trained so well, I could just receive a look from an adult and I knew that there was a necessary response. Just responding in whatever way felt comfortable to me, which many times would be not responding at all, was not acceptable.

SITUATIONS THAT "TALK"

As children of God, I believe that there are proper ways that we should respond to various situations that "talk" to us. We can look at the life of Jesus Christ as a great example of responding in the proper way in those situations. Whether we realize it or not, many situations "talk" to us through the avenue of our thoughts. Let me explain to you what I mean by this by looking at an example of Jesus.

Mark 11:12-14 NKJV
"Now the next day, when they had come out from Bethany, He was hungry. And seeing from afar a fig tree having leaves, He went to see if perhaps He would find something on it. When He came to it, He found nothing but leaves, for it was not the season for figs. In response Jesus said to it, "Let no one eat fruit from you ever again." And His disciples heard it."

Don't you just love how it said *"In response Jesus said to it..."*? In response to what? Jesus responded to the very thought of lack. There were leaves on the fig tree which made it appear that there would be figs on it. Even though it wasn't the season for figs, Jesus still was disappointed, and that disappointment "spoke" to Him. Now of course, the fig tree didn't literally speak to Jesus. However, through the vehicle of His thoughts, it did.

Jesus demonstrated the proper response. We should speak to it!

If we think about it, we've all had challenges that "spoke" to us. How did you respond to them? Did you just ignore those thoughts and hope that they went away? Did you entertain them and start to believe the negative information that was being transmitted to you? Jesus demonstrated the proper response. We should speak to it!

God doesn't want us ignorant of Satan's devices and strategies. Remember that his greatest strategy is to use the power of suggestion. He'll attempt to transmit to you the suggestion of a wrong thought. He does this in hopes that you will receive it, roll that thought over in your mind, and now make it part of your system of thinking. If you allow that thought to become a part of your regular thought life, it will cause you to be troubled. You don't have to be troubled because you can and should refuse to let those wrong thoughts into your life. Make the choice today! Refuse to roll those

Shut the door on those wrong thoughts by making God's Word a part of your system of thoughts. Fill your mouth and your thought life with His thoughts.

wrong thoughts around in your mind. Don't accept them as part of your system of thinking. You keep those wrong thoughts from entering your thought life by refusing to think on them.

Some may be asking right now, *"Is it just that easy? How exactly do I just refuse to think on those thoughts?"* Please don't misunderstand what I'm saying. Wrong thoughts will come. They come to every single person who is alive and has a brain that is functioning. What I am saying is that those thoughts don't have to be permitted to enter into your thought life. When you refuse to think on that wrong thought, you should respond to it by speaking the Word of God. Shut the door on those wrong thoughts by making God's Word a part of your system of thoughts. Fill your mouth and your thought life with His thoughts. You can say that the Bible are His thoughts that have been written down for us.

A COMMON MISTAKE

I believe that the mistake most Christians make is that we try to "out-think" the devil and those toxic thoughts. The mental arena is where he has most of his success with God's children. He attacks our mind in an attempt to try to hold us in the mental arena instead of the arena of faith. If he can hold you in the mental arena, he wins every time. I don't know about you, but I hate to lose. I have too much of the "Winner" Himself in me. Jesus paid too high a price for my victory for me to let the devil have a hold in my life! I'm gonna keep him in the arena of faith so that I win every time!

The way we hold him in the arena of faith is to answer wrong thoughts with the Word of God that we have fed and continue to feed our spirit. Respond to those thoughts with the Word of God and then praise God for His Word. Don't entertain those thoughts that aren't in obedience to the knowledge of Christ. Instead, learn to answer them rather than rolling it over in your mind. Don't give the devil the attention that he wants by getting troubled over those thoughts. What you should do is hold fast to God's word. Keep His Word on your lips, in your heart, and on your mind, and respond accordingly.

"WHAT IF THERE'S DOUBT IN MY HEAD"

Speaking words of faith that we have planted in our hearts is the proper response in every situation. We receive that faith from hearing and believing God's Word. Did you know that faith in your heart will work, even though there is doubt in your head? The reason why is because faith is of the heart, it's not of the head. Understand that and meditate on it. Faith is of the heart, it's not of the head. In other words, it's a spiritual thing. I know sometimes we think that we believe in our heads, but no, it's a spiritual thing.

Mark 11:22&23 (AMPC)

22 And Jesus, replying, said to them, Have faith in God [constantly].

23 Truly I tell you, whoever says to this mountain, Be lifted up and thrown into the sea! and does not doubt at all in his heart but believes that what he says will take place, it will be done for him.

I was meditating on this passage of scripture one day and found another translation that said: "*...and shall not entertain any inner doubt*". Just because those wrong thoughts come to our minds, it doesn't mean that we have to entertain them. Thoughts of fear and doubt will try to enter our hearts, but we don't have to let them. It's when we continue to entertain those thoughts that doubt then gets into our hearts and it becomes the way of life for us.

WHAT ARE YOU FEEDING?

How does faith come? Faith comes by hearing and hearing by the word of God. (Romans

...whatever it is you're feeding more, that's what's going to develop.

10:17) Faith needs to be released. You may have faith in your heart, but that faith needs to be released. You also need to build up that faith, and we do that by hearing the word of God. Faith also needs to be fed. As you feed your faith, your spirit man becomes a lot stronger than your flesh. Anything you feed grows, anything you feed develops. Therefore, whatever it is you're feeding more, that's what's going to develop. If you're feeding your fear, your fear is going to develop. If you're feeding your faith, your faith is going to develop.

This is exactly what happens to many believers because we have not controlled our thought life. When thoughts come, some of them come from God, but there are also thoughts that come from Satan. There are also thoughts about circumstances. When thoughts come in that we do not bring into the obedience of Christ, those thoughts you've let slip can now start to fester in your mind. I will show you how you can overcome wrong thoughts. I would like you to pause your reading for a while and do this quick exercise:

Brain Exercise

In your head, I'd like you to start counting from one to twenty-five. When you get to ten, without stopping your count, I want you to say out loud, "Jesus is Lord! Jesus is Lord of my life! I am full of the Holy Spirit. I am full of God!"

Were you able to get to twenty-five without pausing? Or did you discover that once you started to focus on what you were saying that your mind changed its focus? Therefore, you can bring your thought life into captivity by the words that you say.

MAKE IT SUBMIT!

Thoughts come to me, and I'll be honest with you, I've let some of them fester a bit in the past. Thoughts such as these would come:

- "You're not going to make budget."
- "You are a horrible leader! If people only knew, they wouldn't listen to anything you have to say."
- "Those people don't even like you. You see them laughing over there? They're talking about you!"
- "You're not anointed enough."
- "You don't need to write a book. There are so many good books out there. Why would anyone even pick up a book that you wrote?"

Honestly, the list can go on. However, there have been other times when I became conscious of those thoughts and responded by saying, "No, the word of God says this…". I would respond, *"No, the money will come, praise God! The earth is the Lord's and the fullness thereof."* What was I doing? I was bringing that thought into obedience. I was making it submit. *"No, thought, you can't stay here! Devil, no, you get out of here!"* You bring that thought into obedience because that was a thought that was not in submission. It was not in line, it was not in obedience to Jesus, the anointed One, and His word. It's the enemy's tactic to try and wear you down, to bring fear in your life, to bring worry, to get unbelief in you, and undoubtedly, unbelief is a thief of all God's best blessings.

BUT THESE KIDS…

There are parents who allow worry about their kids to consume them in their minds. Some of you may even be saying right now, *"That's my child! I can't help but worry about them! What do you expect me to do?!"* Have you ever thought about the fact that God can do a better job at raising our kids than we ever can? I'm pretty sure I don't need to state it, but I am in no way saying that we neglect our responsibilities as parents. However, I am saying that we need to have a healthy response to the thoughts that come to us. Does God bring thoughts to us that cause anxiety and stress? No way!

Once you understand that God is not the one sending you that worrisome thought, you say, *"No, I refuse to worry about my kids."* Saying is the aspect of faith that will make it bow to its knees. You want to slap something? Slap that worrying thought. Say what the word says. *"All of my children shall be taught of the Lord and great shall be the peace of my children."* Why is it necessary to respond like this? Here are just a few reasons why:

- *What the enemy wants to do is to construct a stronghold of worry in your life.*
- *This stronghold will then rob you of your peace, your joy, and your rest at night.*

- *It can eventually rob you of your relationship with your children or your spouse.*

These thoughts try to come in, because what the enemy wants to do is to build a stronghold of worry, anxiety, and fear in your life. But praise God, we've been given authority over him, and we have the authority to pull down these vain imaginations, these strongholds.

CHAPTER FIVE
SWAT IT DOWN

I've been told that standing next to the average person, I look extremely tall. At 6'5", I tend to be taller than most of my friends and family. If you are someone that is "vertically challenged", don't start getting jealous because there are challenges that we tall people encounter with our height. For instance, some cities that we fly into do not have airports that can accommodate the larger jets. If we are flying with a commercial airline, it requires us to fly on one of their smaller jets. As I'm walking in you can hear the flight attendant saying, "Sir, please watch your head". I also end up looking so goofy because of how I'm walking and bending all while my bowed head is still grazing the ceiling of that jet. Let's not even talk about how awkward it is if I need to use the tiny restroom at the front of the jet that was not designed with passengers like me in mind.

USE IT TO YOUR ADVANTAGE

My height does have its benefits though so I'm definitely not complaining. When I played basketball, I would use my height and long arms to my advantage for sure. As believers, we have authority that was given to us and that gives us an advantage. We have been given spiritual weapons as a means of attack and counterattack. The weapons that we have been given aren't mediocre weapons, but the Bible tells us that they are mighty in God and it is for a purpose.

2 Corinthians 10:3-5 (AMPC)
3 For though we walk (live) in the flesh, we are not carrying on our warfare according to the flesh and using mere human weapons. 4 For the weapons of our warfare are not physical [weapons of flesh and blood], but they are mighty before God for the overthrow and destruction of strongholds, 5 [Inasmuch as we] refute arguments and theories and reasonings and every proud and lofty thing that sets itself up against the [true] knowledge of God; and we lead every thought and purpose away captive into the obedience of Christ (the Messiah, the Anointed One),

As you read earlier, the real "you" is spirit, but you live in a body made of flesh. I know that when things happen, we want to fight, and we want to fight with our flesh and against whoever is causing us grief or pain. But that is not our fight.

The good fight of faith is not one of the flesh. In Ephesians it says, "*We wrestle not against flesh and blood but against principalities and powers and rulers of the darkness of this world.*" This identifies our enemies as belonging to a category that is different from our natural world. It means then, that we need a different class of weapons to fight such enemies. 2 Corinthians 10:3-5 says, *"For though we walk in the flesh, we do not war after the flesh, for the weapons of our warfare are not carnal."* They are not the same weapons humans use.

> *Satan thrives on ignorance — it's all part of his strategy.*

If we were in a war, I would hate to see a soldier who is out on the frontline without some weapons. Yet, a soldier on the frontline who has some weapons but no ammunition is just as vulnerable. A soldier on the frontline who has some weapons with ammunition but does not know how to pull the trigger will have the same results as the others. You can say that action is the trigger to your faith. A soldier that has all these resources but fails to use them when needed because they were ignorant of what they have, or how to use what they have, will be easy prey.

PROTECT YOURSELF FROM DESTRUCTION

I want to stress again that renewing our minds is so vital to our well-being. When your mind is renewed, the devil can't take advantage of you. You will be one that is not ignorant of the rights and privileges that you possess in Christ. Oh, how Satan thrives on ignorance — it's all part of his strategy. Your Father does not want you to remain ignorant of anything that is wrapped up in the inheritance He prepared for you. In Hosea 4:6, we are told that the people of God are "...*destroyed for a lack of knowledge...*" As you renew your mind, you literally protect yourself from destruction, you protect yourself from failure that comes from remaining ignorant of what God has said to you in His Word. We need to cooperate with God by acting on the Word of God that we feed our spirit. That is how you receive and experience the victory Jesus provided for you.

We need to cooperate with God by acting on the Word of God that we feed our spirit.

THE FIGHT OVER YOUR THOUGHT LIFE

The Apostle Paul tells us that our weapons are not carnal (of the flesh, not natural). We have weapons that are not natural or physical because they are designed to deal with things that are not natural or physical. Namely, imaginations, arguments, theories, and reasoning.

Why should we cast these imaginations down? Because imaginations not dealt with, lead to strongholds in our minds. The fight of your life that I refer to, takes place in the battleground — your mind. The fight of your life is the fight over your thought life. Your thoughts become imaginations and your imaginations become strongholds. In my experiences interacting with people, I have noticed that many times we have a misunderstanding of what strongholds really are. But verse 5 of 2 Corinthians 10 tells us what they are. They are wrong imaginations, wrong thinking, and wrong reasonings that are contrary to the word of God. Wrong ways of thinking are the negative strongholds that you and I deal with.

There is a war waging for your mind; your soul. I hope you realize that it's not that you just have some gray matter floating around in your head to make you go left, go right, do a little robot dance, or moonwalk. But this is where your will and your emotions are. Now, emotions as a whole aren't bad. God gave them to us for a reason. But emotions (especially negative ones) must be brought under subjection, and into obedience to the knowledge of Christ. And so, it is necessary that we "cast down" these imaginations. We can also say "swat down" or "slap down" these imaginations because this is a fight.

> *...imaginations not dealt with lead to strongholds in our minds.*

THROW A "BLOCK PARTY"

Whenever I played basketball and I was on the defensive side of the ball, one of my favorite things to do was to block the shot of an opposing player. Even now, if I'm playing and someone comes and tries to make a basket, they can be coming right at me, but I'm not moving out of the way. I'm jumping up to swat that ball down! It was even better if I swatted the opposing player's shot with authority because it caused them to be intimidated. The next time that I was anywhere near them and defending them, they were afraid to try to shoot again. Even if they did try, they would have to alter their shot to one that wasn't a high-percentage shot. While talking trash, I would sometimes say *"I'm throwing a 'block party' and you're all invited"*. We need to take the same approach with thoughts that are contrary to God's Word. When the devil brings one of his thoughts, swat that thought down so hard that he thinks, "I better not try that thought again".

Maybe you don't play basketball and can't relate, but surely at some point in your life you've had to deal with mosquitoes. If there are mosquitoes flying around me, I'm not just going to let one land on me. What do you think I'm going to do? I'm going to swat it down! I mean you just slap it down. I know some of you have been wanting to just slap something. Well, here is your chance to slap something. I don't mean in the flesh. What I'm talking about are those wrong thoughts that may be coming to you because they can end up being a stronghold in your life.

Paul warns us about *"casting down every*

imagination and every high thing that exalts itself against the knowledge of God, bringing EVERY thought to the obedience of Christ". That means that there are certain thoughts that are not going to necessarily line up with Christ. There are thoughts that do not line up with the will of God for your life. This is why we need to bring every thought into captivity. Just swat it down. If it is a thought that is exalting itself, if it's a thought that's full of pride, if it's a thought that's contrary to the word of God, then it's not God's job to do this, it's our job. The pronoun "you" is understood. The passage is saying, YOU cast down imaginations, YOU cast down every high thing that exalts itself against the knowledge of God and YOU bring into captivity every disobedient thought and YOU make that thought obey Christ. We should not let one disobedient thought escape.

Now be honest, we go through a lot of thoughts throughout the day. And it seems that women deal with more thoughts than men do. I don't know if it's scientifically proven or not, but a wife can be talking to her husband, who appears to be paying attention, but nothing is really going on in his head. Whereas, when a husband talks to his wife, he only needs to make one statement, and her thought pattern, like a switchboard operator, begins to connect all different kinds of things. Her brain begins to say, *"Hold on sir, I'll connect you to this and I'll connect you to that and this is what you mean by this, and this is what you mean by that and I'm just going to grab this from here and do this here and put this there"*. That is the truth whether you want to admit it or not. Men and women are wired differently. Men take the approach, *"Hold on one second……… I got you."* But his wife's brain responds, "Alert, *alert, he's not getting it, let me see if I can change this right here."*

But whether we are male or female, all of us must bring into captivity every thought. We've got to cast them down because they're exalting themselves. We must cast down every thought that is not in line with, or in submission and obedience and agreement to, the anointed One and His word.

NOT ONE IDLE THOUGHT...

We cannot allow even one idle thought to go unchecked. Does every thought matter? Yes, they do. Every thought matters. Then how in the world can we do this? Now what I will tell you is there is a way NOT to deal with it and that is you don't try to outthink that idle thought. In other words, when those thoughts come, you just swat them down. You say, *"No! No! No! This is what the Word says."* Because here is what I do know: words are just a group of letters that are put together to give a thought some substance. Does that make sense? Or let's say it this way, every thought has the power to have form. For instance, if I start to share with you about some construction that I am planning on having done on a building, some of you won't be able to see it yet. But because I've been thinking about it, meditating on it, and speaking about it, I can communicate those thoughts to an architect. So now my architect can use my thoughts to create a vision and a plan for the building I want to construct. From this plan, my building will take on form and substance. A few months later people who could not see it before can now come by and see the completed structure. But it all began with a thought.

The car that you may drive today didn't suddenly appear, but somebody had a thought and focused on it and caused it to become a vision. From that vision, they created a plan, and from that plan, they designed the car. They then went on to build that car and now you can drive that car. But it all began with a thought. Everything that we see began with a thought.

> *Everything that we see began with a thought.*

But when it comes to negative thoughts, you cannot combat those thoughts with just other thoughts. You must do some speaking. Why is it necessary to speak? You must speak because your enemy cannot read your mind. His greatest weapon is the power of suggestion.

He'll try to send certain thoughts to your mind. He wants to get you to entertain those thoughts because he knows that he has no authority over you. He understands that he has no authority over the believer. Christ Himself lives in you! As a born-again believer, God Himself has come and taken up residence on the inside of you. Just think, God, who is all-powerful, is on the inside of you.

Does the devil think that he can touch you? This is what he does. He tries to see what he can get you to agree with or allow. He sends thoughts of lack, thoughts of depression, thoughts of offense, and thoughts of hatred, to try to get you to think on them until they become vain imaginations.

He suggests that perhaps that symptom in your body is a sign of a serious disease, one that took the lives of your mother and sister. He suggests that you are probably going to lose your house because the economy is very bad now. He suggests that the people on your job or in your church don't like you or are jealous of you or don't really care about you. If you don't bring those thoughts into captivity, if you don't slap them down, if you don't swat them down, then what's going to happen is, the more they come in and the more you entertain them, these thoughts will become strongholds.

Now, it doesn't mean that thoughts won't come to your mind. Many thoughts flood our minds in just a few seconds. But these thoughts can become strongholds of fear and doubt. *"Oh, where is the money going to come from now?" "What are we going to do?" "Why does this always happen to me?"* It's because some thoughts that weren't in obedience to the Anointed One, that didn't fall in line and were not submitted to Him and His word, crept in and now you find yourself in the fight of your life.

He says to fight the good fight of faith. He equips us with weapons of warfare that are not carnal, but they are mighty through God for the pulling down of strongholds. By and with these weapons, we swat down and capture every thought that is contrary to God's plan for our lives. 1 Peter 5:7 says, *"Casting the whole of your care [all your anxieties, all your worries, all your concerns, once and for all on Him, for He cares for you affectionately and cares about you watchfully."*

...some thoughts that weren't in obedience to the anointed One, that didn't fall in line and were not submitted to Him and His word, crept in and now you find yourself in the fight of your life.

It talks about casting all of our care upon the Lord for He cares for us. You know, worry will try to come in, fear will try to creep in, but we must cast worry and fear down, and cast our care upon the Lord. All worry is, is meditation on the wrong thing. Therefore, when thoughts of worry come in, you must capture them, you must swat them down, I mean, you just have to get violent with them. It doesn't help if you just think it. You have to say something.

CHAPTER SIX

DON'T FEED THE STRAYS

As you and I feed our faith, our faith becomes stronger. But how do you feed your faith? You feed your faith the same way that it comes, by the Word of God. On the flip side, if you feed your fear, then your fear will become stronger. Whatever it is that you're feeding will become stronger. Additionally, it is imperative to know that we must exercise our faith. That's where the releasing of your faith comes in. You exercise your faith so that you don't become a fat spiritual *"couch potato"*.

Whatever it is that you're feeding will become stronger.

I always wanted pets to the extent that I went overboard with it. I wanted a pet dolphin, pet eagle, pet tiger, pet iguana, pet lizard. In fact, I would have adopted any animal that would have wanted me. The one thing that held me back was that I could not get my parents to agree with me. Thank God, they allowed us to have parakeets. We had some fish and some hamsters, too. I also had a puppy because I thought my mom said that I could have a puppy, and somebody was giving away a puppy, so I brought it home. It was one of those breeds that look like a dog even when it's still a puppy. So, my mom said, *"What are you doing with that dog?"* I said, *"You told me I could have a puppy."*

Of course, she had no recollection of that conversation.

The purpose of the story is to tell you that any animal that came by the house, I wanted to feed it, and then I wanted to keep it. But my mother, being the wise woman that she is, knew that if she allowed me to feed those stray animals, they would keep coming back because they have found a place where someone was going to love them and feed them. And so, you know, even though I didn't like it, if I had my own way, we would have ended up with a zoo at our house. So, she would "shoo" those pets. No, not pets, I'm sorry, I can't call them pets. She would chase those stray dogs or cats. She would send them away because she knew that if we allowed that animal to stay there, it was going to end up living there and there could be certain consequences to my decision.

Thoughts are very similar. If you allow certain thoughts to just come and linger around you, and you feed them, those thoughts will take up residence. Sometimes those thoughts can even look cute, *"Oh that's a cute little thought, look at that thought, can I keep this thought? It's really cute, can I?"* But what we don't realize sometimes is that thought can be disease infested. Just like a raccoon can look cute but it can be carrying rabies, so it is with some seemingly harmless thoughts. Another similarity between thoughts and small animals is that they don't usually stay small, except for those special breeds. How many stories have we heard of people who made pets of snakes and cubs, bears and lions and tigers, only to be destroyed by them when they become full-grown?

Our thoughts are similar. If we allow certain thoughts to stay, if we begin to entertain them, like I was entertaining those animals, playing with them, and feeding them, that thought is going to end up staying there and growing there. Then that thought that even looked cute could end up being disease infested. Not only does it affect you, but it could affect your whole family.

This is how Satan works. He tries to bring thoughts of fear, of doubt, of unbelief, of hatred, of offense, of depression, of worry, to see whether we will feed them, entertain them, and invite them to remain as residents. But in this, the fight of our life, we must bring every thought into obedience.

Every thought is important. I know sometimes we want to think that a thought is just a thought. But thoughts are powerful. The car you may drive or ride in today just didn't suddenly appear. It began as a thought, a concept that turned into a vision, and a vision turned into a plan. That plan turned into or materialized into that car. When an artist looks at a blank canvas, he sees something totally different from what you and I see. Because before he starts painting, he has a thought in his mind of the masterpiece he is about to paint.

You and I as believers must make sure that we win the fight of our thought life and of our words. You see the enemy, the devil, will try to get you to fight him in the arena of mental assent and reasoning but we should fight him in the arena of faith. It's a faith fight. You are not fighting against him, but you're fighting in the arena of faith. In other words, you're saying, *"I'm going to bring every thought into captivity, into obedience."* Sometimes we think that we can just outthink certain thoughts, but you know you can't do that. You know that's not the way to do it. If you try to outthink your thoughts, you'll lose every time. But with your words, you can win every time.

What is a word? A word is just a collection of letters that have been formed together to illustrate a thought. Words are containers of thoughts. It doesn't mean that thoughts won't try to come. You know, one preacher said that you can't stop a bird from flying over your head, but you can stop it from laying a nest in your **hair**. In other words, thoughts would try to come, but you as a believer, you as a person of faith, you as a person who has been given authority in Christ can cast down every vain imagination.

In 2 Corinthians 10:3, the Word of the Lord says, *"For though we walk in the flesh, we do not war after the flesh."* Verse 4 of that same chapter goes on to say that our weapons are not man-made weapons but weapons that are mighty through God, weapons that are able to pull down strongholds. It's important to realize that it's not in your own strength, it's not that you're mighty in your own strength or in your own abilities, but you're mighty through God, to the pulling down of strongholds. Verse 5 says, *"Casting down imaginations and every high thing that exalts itself against the knowledge of God, and bringing it into captivity, every thought to the obedience of Christ."* The Amplified Bible puts it this way, *"for though we walk, live in the flesh, we are not carrying on our warfare according to the flesh, and using mere human weapons, for the weapons of our warfare are not physical weapons of flesh and blood, but they are mighty before God, for the overthrow and destruction of strongholds, in as much as we refute arguments and theories and reasonings, and every proud and lofty thing that sets itself up against the true knowledge of God, we lead every thought and purpose away captive into the obedience of Christ, the Messiah, the anointed one."*

Now, the fight of our life is not with flesh and blood, and our fight is not even with the devil. We're not trying to get victory. When Jesus went down to hell, he defeated the devil and his demons. Remember, Jesus fought that fight for us, and He triumphed over every demonic spirit and fallen angel. He made a show of them openly. That is why at the name of Jesus, every time you mention the name of Jesus, Hell trembles.

I think if we could just really understand and recognize the authority that **we** have, we wouldn't let certain things take place in our lives while we sit idly by. We won't just allow things to have control over us when we understand that God has given us the authority. Didn't Jesus say, *"I give you authority to trample on snakes, and serpents and scorpions?"* When He came back from the dead, before He ascended into heaven, He said, *"All authority has been given unto me, go ye therefore and preach the gospel, lay hands on the sick, cleanse the lepers, raise the dead, cast out demons, these signs shall follow them that believe, they'll speak with new tongues"*.

He could have kept all that authority for Himself, but as soon as He received that authority, He says, *"Go ye therefore..."*. In other words, He transferred or translated that authority to you and me. Aren't you glad about that? We've been given authority over the enemy. Once we understand that he's already a defeated foe, we see our fight from a different perspective. This is how the enemy operates. He brings certain suggestions, certain thoughts to you and if you allow that thought to keep playing in your mind, it becomes a stronghold in your life. Those thoughts now begin to manifest themselves in actions and habits. In the King James Version, verse 5 talks about casting down imaginations and every high thing that exalts itself against the knowledge of God and bringing into captivity every thought. How many thoughts? We are to bring every thought to the obedience of Christ, to the obedience of the Messiah, the Anointed One, and His word.

Once we understand that he's already a defeated foe, we see our fight from a different perspective.

Can there not be certain thoughts that don't fall in line with the will of God for our lives? Do we have thoughts that aren't in obedience with His will, and His purpose for our lives? Where do these thoughts come from? It comes from the enemy when he uses one of his greatest weapons, that of suggestion. He did it with Eve in the Garden of Eden. *"Did God say?"* He did it to the children of Israel,

"Can God provide a table in the desert?" He tried it on Jesus, *"If you are the Son of God, command these stones to become bread."* He uses the same strategy on us. He will bring thoughts to your mind. Stray thoughts like the stray animals I wanted to entertain. Once you entertain the thought, he will send it again and again, encouraging you to feed the thought until it becomes a part of your thought life and when it becomes a part of your thought life, it now can become a stronghold in your life. Therefore, we must capture those thoughts, pull them down, cast down all those vain imaginations, and chase those thoughts away.

You see, our flesh wants to cooperate with the thoughts of the enemy. Have you ever noticed that when you decide to pray or read the Bible, the thought comes to you, *"I'm really tired"*. And almost immediately it's as though something is released in your body to make you feel tired even if you aren't really tired? How do we know that? Because if you turn on the television or begin to scroll through social media, the tiredness immediately evaporates. Isn't that the truth?

The apostle Paul was very aware of the battlefield that exists in our minds. In Romans chapter 12:2, he writes *"and do not be conformed to this world but be transformed by the renewing of your mind that you may prove what is that good and acceptable, and perfect will of God"*. What makes you like this world is when you begin to think like the world thinks. So that's why he's saying here, don't be conformed to this world, but be transformed by the renewing of your mind, and the renewing of the mind is something that should be done every day. Transforming your mind takes in changing your thinking and refusing to entertain or feed the thoughts that come to you seeking your permission to reside in your mind and build a stronghold there. DON'T FEED THOSE STRAYS.

CHAPTER SEVEN
THE POWER OF WORDS

Have you ever seen someone having a wonderful day until one phone call changes everything? How is it possible that from having such a great day they can be plunged into the depths of despondency from the heights of joy by one phone call? The words spoken on that call had the power to change the whole atmosphere for them. Those words that were spoken produced certain thoughts in them and changed their perception of their situation.

We said that words are containers that hold thoughts. Most times the thought comes first and then we say what we have been thinking. But we can also change what we're thinking by what we say, because words, when they're released, create thoughts. You don't just say something and not think about it. We used this illustration before, but I would like to refer to it once more. If I say, "blue car", right away you picture a blue car in your mind. The thought of a blue car is formed in your mind. You don't see the words, "B - L - U - E - C - A - R," but you see a picture of a blue car. It becomes an imagination. The fight of your life is this, bringing into captivity every thought to the obedience of Christ. Every thought is important because the enemy will try to attack you in your thought life. If the words that you speak do not produce in you right thoughts, then you need to change what you have been saying.

The Word of God itself is a manifestation of His thoughts. So now you can think His thoughts every time you read the Word and every time you meditate on the Word of God. We understand that faith comes by hearing and hearing the Word of God. But we also understand that faith without works is dead. You've got to start putting things into practice if faith is going to work for you. This is something no one, not even God, can do for you. He says YOU cast down these vain imaginations. We want to say, *"Oh God, take this thought from me."* No, YOU do it.

How do you do it? Let's imagine that you had a pail of dirty water. What would happen if you were to take a hose and continually pour clean water into that pail of dirty water? Eventually all the dirty water would overflow, and clean water would replace it. Well, it's the same thing with words. We try to outthink our thoughts, but that's like trying to scoop out the dirty water by handfuls. It just makes a mess. Things start to fall apart. But if you would exchange that thought with the word of God and pour the word of God, which is also referred to as water, that bad thought would eventually leave. So that's why this is the fight of our life because you'll always have certain thoughts coming against you, thoughts of fear, thoughts of lack, thoughts of sickness and defeat. You find yourself saying things like, *"Oh where is the money going to come from?*

The word of God itself is a manifestation of His thoughts... you can think His thoughts every time you read the word and every time you meditate on the word of God.

What are we going to do now? I feel like I'm going to be sick again."

When we allow a negative thing to enter our eye gate and into our ear gate, it becomes a part of our thought life, and as it becomes a part of our thought life, if we meditate on it instead of on the word of God, it becomes a stronghold in our lives and those thoughts eventually will become spoken words. Because the more you think on those thoughts, they move to your heart, and out of the abundance of the heart mouth speaks. (Matthew 12:34) And if Jesus really was serious when He said that we can have what we say, if He wasn't just playing around, if He wasn't just using words loosely, then why aren't we being more intentional with our words? Speak the word, change your thought life by speaking the word. Swat that thought down, bring it into subjection, capture it, recognize it, and say, *"No, I resist that thought."* Don't try to outthink it.

If other people are around, you may not want to say loudly, *"Shut up, I don't receive that."* They may want to doubt your sanity. But if you're alone, you can do that. Say something right away to counteract that thought. If the person who spoke the negative word around you is there and you can't think of scripture verses to reverse what they said, you can simply say, *"Oh I'm so glad that since I've accepted Christ in my life, what you said is no longer my lot in life."* And then you can say or paraphrase a verse of scripture that expresses faith in Him. When you do that, you change the focus to what you are now saying. So don't try to outthink it. You'll lose every time because that is the devil's arena. Don't try to fight him in his arena. His arena is the arena of reason. Our arena as believers is the arena of faith. We're not moved by what we see, we're not moved by what we feel, we're not moved by what we hear, but we're moved by faith, we're moved by the word of God. And so, if you want to win the fight of faith, the fight of your life, you must fight him in your arena, the arena of faith.

I heard a story that illustrates what we've been sharing about the importance of fighting in your arena. Pastor Mark Hankins said that he was watching a tv show once and there was a guy in a competition that was so huge that he said to his son Aaron, *"Look at how strong that guy is, even his muscles have muscles, I sure won't like to get into a fight with that guy."* But as they continued to watch the show, part of the competition involved getting into the water and as soon as that big guy got into the water, he started to splash around and flounder. Pastor Mark said, *"When I saw that I started laughing because if that guy ever wanted to fight me, I would hit him hard and then jump in the pool."* He knew if that big guy came into that arena, He would win. He could drown that big guy with all his muscles. Always maintain your fight in the arena of faith!

CHAPTER EIGHT

WHO IS CONTROLLING YOUR SOUL?

I've said for years when speaking to young people and adults alike that *"every decision leads to a destination."* In other words, the decisions we make in our lives today will determine the destination that we arrive at in our future. One day, many years ago, I was listening to a message on faith by Bro. Kenneth E. Hagin and he made a statement that caused me to take an evaluation of my life of faith. I would like to share that statement with you and hope that you will also do your own evaluation of your life of faith.

> *"If our confession is wrong it's because our believing is wrong. If our believing is wrong it is just because our thinking is wrong. And if our thinking is wrong it is because our minds have not been renewed with the Word of God and we're not thinking in line with God's holy Word."*   *-Kenneth E. Hagin*

You see, wrong thinking produces wrong believing. Wrong believing produces wrong speaking. Wrong speaking eventually leads you to a place of choosing a wrong decision or action. If we were to take some time to look back over our lives, we would find times when we made decisions that were great and other times when we made decisions that were destructive. I hope that by now you feel as though you are empowered to live the life of victory that God has called you to live. As a matter of fact, I don't want you to just feel like you are, I want you to know that you are and start walking in it.

Can you picture a life filled with all the goodness of God? Imagine a life where you never take wrong turns or make decisions that lead to disaster. Imagine a life where you always hear the voice of God and follow it accurately. This doesn't have to sound "too good to be true" because we can have a life just like this.

In the life of a functioning human being, there isn't a day that goes by that isn't filled with a bunch of choices and decisions. Every single day we make a plethora of choices and decisions. Many of the choices we make are deliberate while others are subconsciously made based on how we were preconditioned. If we were to take a look at Deuteronomy chapter 28, we would see that every choice that we make falls into the category of Life or

Death. I'd like to also add that NOT making a decision still qualifies as making a decision.

Many of the choices we make are deliberate while others are subconsciously made based on how we are preconditioned.

YOU CHOOSE

We really can say that the life that we are experiencing right now is a result of the choices we have made. As sovereign as God is, the choices we make are what will determine a "life of blessing" or a "life of cursing". Unfortunately, most people choose to live their life blaming other people or things rather than taking responsibility for where they are. The Bible shows us that our life is a product of the choices (good or bad) that we have made.

I remember as a kid hearing a preacher tell a joke about someone that saw the devil crying uncontrollably in a corner somewhere. (Please understand that this is a joke and only being used for illustration purposes.)

Jim: What's wrong devil?
Satan: I'm just really sad right now...
Jim: Is it because churches are being built?
Satan: (still crying) No...
Jim: Is it because you feel like you're losing to God?
Satan: No, I know that I've already lost...
Jim: Well then, why are you crying?
Satan: I'm crying because God's kids keep lying on me and blaming me for everything bad that happens to them... even things that I didn't do!

Please don't misunderstand what I'm saying by sharing this illustration with you. I am in no way implying that we don't have an adversary. Satan is bad and God is good. No question about it! We do, however, need to recognize that the decisions we make take us closer to a particular destination.

That's why we have no business making decisions that have been influenced by Satan, the deceiver. Understanding how to make right choices is critical and it is certainly necessary that we understand the process.

UNDERSTANDING YOU...

The Word of God reveals to us the three-fold nature of man. We understand that we are spirit, (that is who we are, the real us), we possess a soul, and we live in a body. In 1 Thessalonians 5:23, we read *"...may your whole spirit, soul, and body be preserved blameless...".*

I Thessalonians 5:23 NKJV
Now may the God of peace Himself sanctify you completely; and may your whole spirit, soul, and body be preserved blameless at the coming of our Lord Jesus Christ.

You really can read that as, "may your whole spirit, (whole) soul, and (whole) body..." With our spirit, we contact God, the spirit realm, and things of the spirit. Your soul is the seat of your emotions, your mind, and your will. The eternal part of you, your spirit and your soul, are housed in your body.

In other words, the body is our house, and with our body, we contact the physical world. We contact the physical world through our five senses, taste, touch, sight, hearing, and smell. The Bible says, to be absent from the body, is to be present with the Lord. (2 Corinthians 5:8) Should Jesus tarry, the body will return to dust when someone dies. You don't take your body with you when you leave here.

When we talk about the soul, we are referring to the mind, the emotions, and the will. Whenever you make a decision, you are exercising your will on the basis of the interaction that happens between your mind and your emotions. Through your senses (what you see, hear, touch, taste, and feel), your intellect gathers and evaluates all the information that is coming to you. What then occurs is that you emotionally "feel" certain ways about certain situations. Based on the interaction that took place between your evaluation (intellectually) and your response (emotionally), you then make a choice as you operate your will.

THE COMMITTEE OF YOUR SOUL

The majority of the time, our soul operates on a subconscious level and we're just not really aware of it. The more aware we are, the more we can exercise some control. Think of your soul as a committee. The "committee of your soul" comes together to have a meeting and all three parts interact with each other. It is where what you think *(the mind/intellect)* interacts with what you feel *(your emotions),* and the end result is a choice made to act *(your will).*

Every decision leads you to a destination. What is it then that fuels the vehicle of your decisions? The fuel for your decisions can be found in your desire. Desire will always precede a decision. Desires are produced when your ability to think interacts with your feelings. Usually, when what you're thinking interacts with what you're emotionally feeling, whichever is more dominant between the two will determine your decision. You will not have a strong desire and then make an opposite decision of that desire.

Whatever is the most dominant influence over your thoughts and feelings is the controlling factor in your decision-making process. The most influential "member" of the "committee of your soul" will have its way.

Allow me to break it down a little more...

Say for instance you've paid a lot of money for an all-inclusive trip and it is non-refundable. You have a flight to catch but you're really tired. You would really love to sleep in for a few more hours. It actually "feels" great to sleep in more, but your mind starts thinking, *"If I don't get up right now, I could miss my flight and lose all that money I paid."* Because your desire to not forfeit this trip is stronger than your feelings of how great it would be to stay in bed a little longer, you make a choice for "blessing" rather than "cursing" and you get your body out of the bed. This is how the soul works. Whichever part of you is most influential, whichever part is strongest, that is what will control you.

The most influential "member" of the "committee of your soul" will have its way.

Here's another example that may hit a little closer to home. Let's say that I'm feeling a lot of irritation and anger towards somebody. They just happened to hurt me recently and I am still having some feelings of unforgiveness towards them. I really would rather not be around them nor do I feel like being friendly towards them. But I am a believer and I have made the decision to let the love of God rule in my life. Because I have fed my spirit and have enough of the Word of God in my mind, I think, "*I need to show myself friendly and be loving. I need to expect them to respond to my actions rather than me responding to theirs. I can be gentle, kind, and I will believe the best.*"

If I have been thinking more about my negative feelings than about what the Word tells me to do, even though I may know better, those strong feelings I entertained would dominate my behavior. Always remember, the part of you that is strongest, the part of you that is most influential, that is the part that will control you.

VARIOUS ROLES IN THE COMMITTEE

The Role of the Mind

The quality of the life that you are currently experiencing is a direct result of what you have been doing with your mind. The decisions that you have been making on a daily basis is what will determine your quality of life. This book which you are now reading is a product of the decisions that I had to make to discipline myself to sit down to write it. I had to battle the thoughts that tried to discourage me from doing what I sensed in my heart to do. When the mind is not being fed the proper information, decisions for life and blessing will not happen. I had to constantly feed my mind the information that was needed to get me to a place that would cause me to decide to start and continue with this book. Whenever I failed to do so, there would be no motivation to complete what I started and intended to finish.

The Role of the Emotions

Emotions don't have to always be labeled as a bad thing. God has actually designed us with emotions to cause us to have momentum toward the things that we have set out to do. Emotions are the part of that committee that has given us the capacity to "feel". The emotions that we experience are the result of what we have meditated on. If we were to think in terms of cause and effect, rolling thoughts around in your mind would be the cause and your emotions would be the effect.

Cause: thoughts meditated on
Effect: the emotions we experience

What we consistently think about along with the words we constantly speak will ultimately give direction to what we feel emotionally. When it comes to God's plan for your life, do you realize that He actually wants us to feel excitement? God wants us to be enthusiastic and determined about what He has called us to do! In order to feel that passion and determination, we have to make the practice of thinking about His plans and purposes for us, along with His power towards us. The more we do this, the more the capacity of our emotions produces the momentum needed to take us towards the direction of our God-given destiny.

CHAPTER NINE

THE UNCONTROLLED SOUL

It has been said that whatever controls your soul controls your destiny. Now, that "control" could also read "influence". In other words, whatever influences your soul influences your destiny. If you allow the enemy to influence your soul, he can ultimately determine the outcome of your destiny. Similarly, if religious traditions influence your soul, then they're controlling your destiny. These influences, be they good or bad, can come from the devil, religious traditions, circumstances, other people, or even God. If your idea of God is that He is out to get you, then that's what's going to control your destiny. If you're allowing circumstances to control your soul, then they're what's going to control your destiny. Whatever controls your soul controls your destiny.

HEY YOU...

I'd like to remind you that when I'm referring to YOU, I'm wanting you to understand that the real you is spirit. You are a recreated human spirit made in the image and likeness of God Himself. That's the part of you that connects with God. Therefore, since the real you is a spirit, your spirit should dictate to the soul and body what you want them to do.

Many times, in the Body of Christ we get it mixed up because we use a lot of religious language. So, when thirty people respond to an invitation to receive Jesus as their Savior, we say that thirty souls came into the kingdom. What really took place is that thirty spirits were born again and made alive in Christ. I understand that because of the terminology that we use, we tend to think that spirit and soul are the same, but they are not. Hebrews 4:12 tells us that the word of God is able to divide spirit and soul. Now if your spirit man controls your soul, if your spirit man controls your thinking, your will, your emotions, then your spirit man is going to control your destiny. We've already learned that one of the greatest strategies of the enemy is the power of suggestion. The devil has no authority over you except what you allow. James 4:7 says, "Resist the devil and he will flee from you". In other words, if you don't resist him, then he has a place to come into your life. He's going to try to show up. He walks about as a roaring lion seeking whom he may devour. It does not say that he is a roaring lion but he's like a roaring lion. Why do lions roar? They do so to strike terror on their prey, to paralyze and disarm them. The devil also makes a lot of noise and goes around to see whom he can get. But the bible says, resist him, steadfast in your faith. When you resist him, the Bible says, he will flee from you. Now, if you look up that word flee in the dictionary, it means "to run from as in terror". We are not to allow him to hang around trying to negotiate. No, the Passion Translation says we are to *"take a decisive stand against him and resist his every attack with strong, vigorous faith" (1 Peter 5:9)*.

> *We are not to allow him (the devil) to hang around trying to negotiate.*

If you don't recognize the devil's tactics, you won't know how to resist him. He comes in the form of fear. Fear is not of God, it's of the devil. If you resist fear, it will flee from you. Doubt is not of God, it's of the enemy. If you resist doubt, it must flee from you. Sickness is not of God, it's from the enemy. If you resist sickness, it must flee from you.

The battlefield and the fight of our life is really the fight over the soul because you've already been born again, your spirit has already been born again, you're a brand-new creature in Christ. But do you realize that you still have your mind that needs to be renewed daily? The Bible says in Romans Chapter 12:1; it says, *"I beseech you therefore brethren by the mercies of God that you present your bodies a living sacrifice."* So, our bodies need to be presented daily. We also still have our flesh to deal with. That's why the Word asks us to present it as *"a living sacrifice holy and acceptable unto God, which is your reasonable service"*. Verse 2 goes on to say, *"and do not be conformed to this world but be transformed"*. So, a transformation needs to take place. How does this transformation come about? By the renewing of the mind. We are believers. Our spirits have been born again, but we still have our flesh to deal with, and we still have our minds to deal with.

Both our flesh and our souls (in need of being renewed) are opposed to what has taken place in our spirits. Our flesh wants to control our soul. Our flesh wants to tell our souls how to feel, and how to respond to the temptations and testing on the outside. But our regenerated spirit can also tell the soul what to do. David spoke to his soul in Psalm 42:11 saying, "Why my soul, are you downcast?" It's healthy to talk to your soul when it is wanting to act up.

INFORMATION INPUT

Your soul is constantly receiving information from your spirit and your body that are measuring and evaluating. I can't stress enough how important it is to make decisions that you believe are consistent with the will of God. The more you meditate on those decisions and get emotionally involved, the more momentum will build and move you towards that direction.

Someone with an uncontrolled soul will think and respond out of the natural arena. That's because of what is more dominant. They will react simply to what signals they receive from their natural senses. That individual will give more creditability to the natural consideration.

Someone with an uncontrolled soul will think and respond out of the natural arena.

Going back to what I shared with you earlier in this book about that particular trial that Lynette and I dealt with her first time giving birth, we sure were tempted to act just out of the natural arena. An uncontrolled soul will cause one to eventually live a life of torment. This is why we need to give attention to controlling our soul.

Lynette and I went through a period of days, weeks, months, and even years of working on controlling our soul. I want to remind you that after two of the seizures Lynette experienced that day, there were a flood of thoughts and even symptoms that she felt in her body. We were greatly tempted to give more credibility to the natural consideration rather than what God said in His Word.

I want to share an experience that we had with you that can help to show how important it is for you to control your soul. Around four years later, Lynette was getting ready to give birth to our son Ethan. Her OBGYN recommended and scheduled a C-Section for this birth. Lynette by this time had given attention to what thoughts she entertained, although there were still battles in her mind throughout.

We had a good night's rest in a hotel near the hospital the night before and Lynette had not been experiencing any alarming challenges. Closer to the time of delivery, they wanted to monitor her closely in order to be ready for anything that may come. On that scheduled day, we arrive early in the morning at the time that they told us to. As we got checked in at the hospital and placed in our room where we would be for the next couple of days, everything seemed to be going ok.

The nurse inserted an IV into Lynette's hand and placed all the different monitors for her and our unborn baby on her body. That nurse then hung a bag of Intravenous Fluids on top of the IV pole next to my wife's bed and then walked out. After maybe a minute or two, Lynette started to panic a little and said to me:

> *"Hun…. I'm feeling the same thing as last time again…"*

She's communicating to me that she is experiencing the same feeling she had before the first and second seizure. You can see the look of fear and concern all over her face as she doesn't want to have this experience again. I want you to notice how crafty Satan is. We were having no complications at all during the pregnancy and now suddenly this is happening — or so she thought.

I lovingly smiled at my beautiful wife who is full of the Spirit of God and the Word of God and made a statement that would transform everything immediately. I would love to tell you that this was a word straight from heaven and filled with so much revelation that even the angels longed to look into it, but it wasn't that. I just simply looked at her with all the love I could show on my face and said these words:

> "Babe, they didn't even hook up anything to the IV..."

She looked at her hand and then noticed that what I said was true and she said, "Ohhhh......". We both immediately started to laugh. It's amazing how fast that same "feeling" she had before the seizures four years prior left her body. It wasn't long after that the procedure took place without a single problem.

Can you see how powerful thoughts that come to you can be? What if Lynette was given time to dwell on the flood of thoughts that attempted to torment her in that case? She would've had to deal with the challenges of an uncontrolled soul. Although I was there to help her, I do believe that even if I wasn't there she would've still walked victoriously. I believe so because of how she had made the practice of feeding her spirit with God's Word and allowing it to dominate.

SYSTEM OVERLOAD

Someone with an uncontrolled soul doesn't even attempt to control thoughts when they come. They just accept whatever thought comes and "feels" real. If I was in that room with someone who had an uncontrolled soul, it wouldn't matter what I said to them if they chose to believe what they "felt" instead.

If you want to make sure that you avoid having an uncontrolled soul, you will have to cast down wrong thoughts or imaginations. You cannot afford to let the random rush of thoughts that are generated mostly by the world dominate your thinking. If you do, the result will be a life of decisions that are dominated by wrong information and feelings. What I've noticed in my experiences is that we have a bunch of believers that want to make decisions according to God's will, but they have an excess of information from the world. Their path tends to be full of turmoil because they can't seem to make the right choices. This is because they don't have enough input of the right information but instead have been overloading their system with the wrong information.

You cannot afford to let the random rush of thoughts that are generated mostly by the world dominate your thinking

REJECTION

I was recently traveling alone and sat on a flight next to someone that I met for the first time and they began to open up to me about how rejection affected them throughout their life. They shared with me how the rejection that they experienced from way back in their childhood affected all their relationships and how important it was that they broke free from it.

I found it interesting that they said that because of an absent father who left when they were a little child, so many lying thoughts came to them over the years. Because they never learned how to properly deal with those thoughts, for years it affected them, from their relationship with their spouse to even with their pastor. Something as simple as their pastor attempting to correct a way of thinking lovingly and biblically, it was received as condemnation. We should never confuse God's correction with condemnation! Thank God this person was able to finally overcome this challenge and said that it has made everything better.

We should never confuse God's correction with condemnation!

We have seen marriages affected negatively because of one spouse attempting to have the other try to fulfill a role that only Jesus can fulfill. Your spouse, though they can be a great representation of Jesus, can never fill the role that only He is to fill in your life. If you don't learn to exchange some of the thoughts, imaginations, and strongholds that you have allowed to stay due to trauma you have experienced in your life, it will be impossible for you to truly see your way out.

The kingdom of darkness works hard to influence your decisions through your body. On the other hand, God works to influence you through your spirit by His Word and His Spirit. If God controls your soul, then He will determine your destiny. You will have to make room for Him to do that.

CHAPTER TEN

BUILDING A SAFE
STRONGHOLD

Earlier in this book I made the statement that we can build a strong, safe, and proper stronghold in our minds through thinking the right thoughts and getting it into our imagination. There is so much safety in this position.

In most Christian circles, the phrase stronghold is thought of in a negative light. While there are negative strongholds that are developed in the lives of people, there is also another side to the coin. The word stronghold is actually a military term. A stronghold is an area that has been fortified in order to protect against an attack. Wise kings would make plans and follow through to build fortified walls around their cities making them very difficult for an enemy to penetrate. Strongholds were intentionally built and took time and effort to build. You can also look at many old castles around the world and see that they were built on high places. This was done to protect and control the strategic flows of resources. Many fortresses were built near a bay or a river to control the traffic either entering or leaving a harbor.

Strongholds were intentionally built and took time and effort to build.

Though it may be true in some cases where sin, sickness, or depression comes as a result of a demonic stronghold in one's life, the Bible teaches that we can also build Godly strongholds. These Godly strongholds are fortified positions in our lives and with them, we can withstand and counter the strategies and attacks of the devil.

When I was in my late teenage years, I began to learn more about my identity in Christ. That time was the starting place for me in a lifelong journey of building a Godly stronghold in this new identity. I am so thankful for the revelation of who I am in Christ! It has been a game-changer in my walk with the Lord.

In 2 Corinthians 5:17 Paul says,

"Therefore, if anyone is in Christ, he is a new creation; old things have passed away; behold, all things have become new."

Prior to that time, I had lived most of my life not knowing who I was. You must understand as a

Pastor's kid, though I had good parents in my life, and we were blessed to be involved in ministry to such wonderful people, no church is perfect. There were statements said to me and made over my life by a few church people that the enemy would use to replay those lies about who he said I was. That, along with my own negative thoughts, was an attempt to build a negative stronghold in me. That stronghold was designed to keep me from experiencing the truth of who I am. I notice now that my walk with God was limited because of my improper view of who I was and even God's love towards me. Ultimately, this was Satan's plan to stop God's plans and purpose for my life.

AN IDENTITY CRISIS

Many people go through life never really finding their true identity. How many times have we heard people all around the world struggling with not knowing who they are? Even within the Body of Christ, many have allowed various things that have happened to them to dictate what they think of themselves and even how they approach life in general.

It is necessary that we build godly strongholds in our lives and one necessary revelation to build is on who you are in Christ. Your identity in Christ Jesus is stronger than any other identification that you can embrace in your life.

...what happened to Jesus is way greater than anything that has ever happened to you!

If your identity is found only in your race, nationality, career, social status, or even with a problem that you have had, you are being severely limited. Just because something happened to you in your past does not mean that is who you are! Satan will try to get you to agree with his view of you and attempt to make it part of your identity. Those past events may have had a great impact on your life, but I am writing to tell you that what happened to Jesus is way greater than anything that has ever happened to you!

STAY OUT OF THE DITCH

Many times, we can get to a place in our lives where we feel stuck. Yes, we may have made mistakes in the past but for us to move forward we are going to have to do just that, MOVE FORWARD knowing that God has a destination for us to reach. Have you ever been driving and seen a car that has gone off the road and into a ditch? That driver had a plan to make it to their destination when they first started on their commute. It could be that the driver was driving under the influence of a controlled substance or maybe they were just distracted or even weary.

On the road of this journey that we call life, there will be multiple opportunities to get over and get stuck in the ditch. You will be offered the *"controlled substance"* of guilt, shame, anxiety, and fear, just to name a few. You may also get distracted or weary of the disappointments that you will encounter in life. Don't allow yourself to get stuck!

Isaiah 43:18-19 (Message)
Forget about what's happened; don't keep going over old history. Be alert, be present. I'm about to do something brand-new. It's bursting out! Don't you see it? There it is! I'm making a road through the desert, rivers in the badlands.

Stop going over old history over and over again! Forget about what has happened! In our brains, there are ditches that we may have gotten stuck in but there is a way to get out! You can get out of that ditch through what the Bible calls sanctification. In speaking of sanctification, one generic meaning of the word is *"the state of proper functioning."* To sanctify someone or something is to set that person or thing apart for the use intended by its designer. For example, a pen is *"sanctified"* when used to write. In the theological sense, things are sanctified when they are used for the purpose God intends. Therefore, a human being is sanctified when he or she lives according to God's design and purpose.

This process of sanctification occurs when we daily acknowledge and take note of the reality of our union with Christ. In John 17:17, Jesus prayed, *"Lord sanctify them by your truth. Your Word is truth."* This is how we build Godly strongholds—with the truth of who we are, which is found in the Word of God. We need to offer every part of us daily and continually, which includes our minds, continually to the dominion of the Spirit of God.

Ephesians 4:23 AMPC
And be constantly renewed in the spirit of your mind [having a fresh mental and spiritual attitude],"

This is how we build Godly strongholds— with the truth of who we are which is found in the Word of God.

STAY FRESH IN YOUR MENTAL ATTITUDE

Satan is always working against your mind and so many times it happens so subtly. Have you ever asked yourself at some point after you made a bad decision *"What was I thinking?"* The devil will always try to find a way in areas where there is lacking a fortified stronghold. Your faith can be subtly eroded if you do not guard and keep your mind in the right place where God and His Word is concerned. That is why we must maintain a fresh mental attitude. We are transformed by the renewing of our minds and the more consistent we are to do so, we build the Godly strongholds that are necessary to win the fight of our life. Your thinking is directly connected to your life of faith.

Ephesians 4:20-24 MSG
"But that's no life for you. You learned Christ! My assumption is that you have paid careful attention to him, been well instructed in the truth precisely as we have it in Jesus. Since, then, we do not have the excuse of ignorance, everything—and I do mean everything— connected with that old way of life has to go. It's rotten through and through. Get rid of it! And then take on an entirely new way of life—a God-fashioned life, a life renewed from the inside and working itself into your conduct as God accurately reproduces his character in you."

If you're going to build a fortified stronghold that protects, it will take a constant renewal of your mind. Everything with your old way of life has to go and you must take on an entirely new way of life. That means the way you thought and even the way you communicate must change.

Philemon 6 says that when we acknowledge every good thing which is in us in Christ, our faith will become effective. God wants to do a work in your mind and imagination and a great way that we allow Him to do so is as we acknowledge how He sees us in Christ. We have a new life in Christ and this life comes with a new way of thinking which brings a completely new lifestyle. Whatever you struggled with in your past will be no more!

In the past, I struggled with thoughts of shame. I've been born-again since I was a little boy yet for so many years, I didn't understand who I was in Christ. As I started to agree with what God said about me and acknowledge with my words what He said, my life was changed forever. I found out that I was made the righteousness of God in Christ (2 Cor. 5:21). Instead of trying to be righteous, I received revelation from God that I was already righteous! I'm not trying to be, I am! Jesus became the embodiment of sin so that I can be the embodiment of righteousness. Glory to God! It wasn't dependent on what I did but was based on what He became for me.

Little did I know at that time that I was actually building a godly stronghold in my mind to protect me from thoughts of being unrighteous along with thoughts of guilt and shame. I would begin to acknowledge this truth of being made the righteousness of God in Christ. I would say, *"Thank you Lord for becoming sin for me... for making me righteous. You placed me in right standing with you and I can approach you as if I never sinned!"* The more I acknowledged that the more effective my faith in that area became.

(For further study I highly recommend you read the books "Taking Your Place In Christ" and "The Power of Identification In Christ" which are both written by Mark Hankins and also "In Him" by Kenneth E. Hagin)

A STRONGHOLD IN THE DAY OF TROUBLE

Nahum 1:7 NKJV
"The Lord is good, A stronghold in the day of trouble; And He knows those who trust in Him."

Have you placed your trust in Him? Have you found your place in Him? Our Lord is good, and He is a stronghold in times of trouble! You must see yourself as God sees you. Sin and affliction in your life has come to an end! In Nahum 1:9 it says, "*He will make an utter end of it and that affliction will not rise up a second time.*" According to 2 Corinthians 5:17, you are a new creation in Christ and your past is finished and gone and everything has become new. That tells us that the power that was released in the death, burial, and resurrection of Christ has brought old things to an end. Hallelujah! The devil is an accuser, and he must be silenced. The enemies of anxiety, fear, shame, and guilt will never rise again and come back to torment you. You've put your trust in the blood of Jesus and in what God has done for you when He sent His Son to take your place. God has a great plan for your life, and you must believe it!

Reading this book may be a start on this journey for some. For others, it may serve as a reminder to elevate you to a higher level. Wherever you are on this journey of life, this book will not serve as a substitute. You must endeavor to continue to develop your fellowship with God and His Word. Meditate on scriptures that are the answer to what you're needing and believing for. As you do, it will cause you to build a strong foundation. It will empower you to build a fortified stronghold with the truth found in His Word. Though there is a fight to faith, always remember that it is a good fight. It's one that we win as we keep our mind on the truth of God's Word and maintain an attitude of faith.

CHAPTER ELEVEN
CONFESSIONS FOR A HEALTHY SOUL

The Bible tells us in 3rd John and verse 2 that God desires that we prosper and be in health as our soul prospers. The level of our prospering happens to be in direct relation to how well our soul prospers. In this chapter, I have included a few confessions along with some scripture references as an example of some ammunition you can use in this fight of faith. Feel free to utilize them for your own life but remember that they are only examples. Read the scripture references for yourself and take time to meditate on them. As you study the Word of God, you will find that there are many more that you can add to your arsenal.

You will notice that there are some scriptures that will include a confession. There are others that will include blank lines. I encourage you to think of what that scripture is saying to you and write down a personal confession in relation to it.

The Great confession of Christ Jesus:

*I believe in my heart that Jesus Christ died on the cross for my sin and unrighteousness. I believe that God raised Him from the dead, and I confess with my mouth that Jesus Christ is Lord. Jesus is my Lord. (**Romans 10:9, 10**)*

Who I am in Christ Jesus: (Samples of personalized confessions of faith)

I have been born again. God is my very own Father, and I

am His very own child.
(Romans 8:14, 15)

I am a new creature in Christ Jesus. Old things are passed away; behold, all things are new.
(II Corinthians 5:17)

I am complete in my union in Christ Jesus, who is the head of all principality and power.
(Colossians 2:10)

I have been made the righteousness of God in Christ Jesus.
(II Corinthians 5:21)

I am God's masterpiece. He has created me new in Christ Jesus! **(Ephesians 2:10)**

What I can do in Christ Jesus:

"I can do all things through Christ who strengthens me."
Philippians 4:13

My Confession of faith:

_____

_____

_____

_____

"For it is God who works in you both to will and to do for His good pleasure." **Philippians 2:13**

My Confession of faith:

_____

_____

_____

_____

"Now thanks be to God who always leads us in triumph in Christ, and through us [d]diffuses the fragrance of His knowledge in every place." **II Corinthians 2:14**

My Confession of faith:

_____

_____

_____

_____

"There is therefore now no condemnation to those who are in Christ Jesus, who[a] do not walk according to the flesh, but according to the Spirit. 2 For the law of the

166

Spirit of life in Christ Jesus has made me free from the law of sin and death." **Romans 8:1-2**

My Confession of faith:

_____

_____

_____

_____

"I can say unto this mountain, Be thou removed, and be thou cast into the sea; and I do not doubt in my heart. I believe that those things that I say shall come to pass. I will have whatever I say. Therefore, when I pray, whatever things I ask, I believe I receive them and I have them." **Mark 11:23-24**

My Confession of faith:

_____

_____

_____

_____

What I have in Christ Jesus:

"And my God shall supply all your need according to His riches in glory by Christ Jesus." **Philippians 4:19**

My Confession of faith:

_____

_____

_____

_____

"The LORD is my shepherd; I have all that I need." **Psalm 23:1 NLT**

My Confession of faith:

_____

_____

_____

_____

The LORD is my light and my salvation so why should I be afraid? The LORD is my fortress, protecting me from danger, so why should I tremble? **Psalm 27:1 NLT**

My Confession of faith:

_____

_____

_____

_____

*"For God has not given us a spirit of fear and timidity,
but of power, love, and self-discipline."*
II Timothy 1:7 NLT

My Confession of faith:

_____

_____

_____

_____

*And this is what God has testified: He has given us
eternal life, and this life is in his Son. Whoever has the
Son has life; whoever does not have God's Son does not
have life.*
I John 5:11, 12 NLT

My Confession of faith:

_____

_____

_____

_____

"But you belong to God, my dear children. You have already won a victory over those people, because the Spirit who lives in you is greater than the spirit who lives in the world." **1 John 4:4 NLT**

My Confession of faith:

_____

_____

_____

_____

Scriptures of God's Peace for Me:

"Don't worry about anything; instead, pray about everything. Tell God what you need and thank him for all he has done. Then you will experience God's peace, which exceeds anything we can understand. His peace will guard your hearts and minds as you live in Christ Jesus. "
Philippians 4:6-7 NLT

170

My Confession of faith:

_____

_____

_____

_____

"And now, dear brothers and sisters, one final thing. Fix your thoughts on what is true, and honorable, and right, and pure, and lovely, and admirable. Think about things that are excellent and worthy of praise. Keep putting into practice all you learned and received from me— everything you heard from me and saw me doing. Then the God of peace will be with you." **Philippians 4:8-9 NLT**

My Confession of faith:

_____

_____

_____

_____

"The LORD gives his people strength. The LORD blesses them with peace." **Psalm 29:11 NLT**

My Confession of faith:

_____

_____

_____

_____

*"'For the mountains may move and the hills disappear, but even then my faithful love for you will remain. My covenant of blessing will never be broken," says the Lord, who has mercy on you." **Isaiah 54:10 NLT***

My Confession of faith:

_____

_____

_____

_____

*"Now may the God of hope fill you with all joy and peace in believing, that you may abound in hope by the power of the Holy Spirit." **Romans 15:13 NKJV***

My Confession of faith:

_____

_____

_____

_____

"For the kingdom of God is not eating and drinking, but righteousness and peace and joy in the Holy Spirit."
Romans 14:17

My Confession of faith:

_____

_____

_____

_____

Scriptures of God's love for Me:

"For God so loved the world that He gave His only begotten Son, that whoever believes in Him should not perish but have everlasting life. For God did not send His Son into the world to condemn the world, but that the world through Him might be saved." **John 3:16-17**

My Confession of faith:

_____

_____

_____

_____

"But God is so rich in mercy, and he loved us so much, that even though we were dead because of our sins, he gave us life when he raised Christ from the dead. (It is only by God's grace that you have been saved!) For he raised us from the dead along with Christ and seated us with him in the heavenly realms because we are united with Christ Jesus." *Ephesians 2:4-6 NLT*

My Confession of faith:

_____

_____

_____

_____

"Give ALL your WORRIES and CARES to God, for He cares about YOU." *1 Peter 5:7 NLT*

My Confession of faith:

_____

_____

_____

"God saved you by his grace when you believed. And you can't take credit for this; it is a gift from God. 9 Salvation is not a reward for the good things we have done, so none of us can boast about it. 10 For we are God's masterpiece. He has created us anew in Christ Jesus, so we can do the good things he planned for us long ago". **Ephesians 2:8-10 NLT**

My Confession of faith:

_____

_____

_____

_____

"But now you have been united with Christ Jesus. Once you were far away from God, but now you have been brought near to him through the blood of Christ." **Ephesians 2:13 NLT**

My Confession of faith:

_____

_____

_____

_____

"Every single moment You are thinking of me! How precious and wonderful to consider that You cherish me constantly in Your EVERY THOUGHT! O God, Your desires toward me are more than the grains of sand-on every shore! When I awake each morning, You're still with me." **Psalms 139:17-18 TPT**

My Confession of faith:

_____

_____

_____

_____

"What shall we say about such wonderful things as these? If God is for us, who can ever be against us? Since he did not spare even his own Son but gave him up for us all, won't he also give us everything else?" **Romans 8:31-32 NLT**

My Confession of faith:

_____

_____

_____

_____

"Can anything ever separate us from Christ's love? Does it mean he no longer loves us if we have trouble or calamity, or are persecuted, or hungry, or destitute, or in danger, or threatened with death? No, despite all these things, overwhelming victory is ours through Christ, who loved us." **Romans 8:35-37 NLT**

My Confession of faith:

_____

_____

_____

_____

And I am convinced that nothing can ever separate us from God's love. Neither death nor life, neither angels nor demons, neither our fears for today nor our worries about tomorrow—not even the powers of hell can separate us from God's love. No power in the sky above or in the earth below—indeed, nothing in all creation will ever be able to separate us from the love of God that is revealed in Christ Jesus our Lord." **Romans 8:38-39 NLT**

My Confession of faith:

_____

_____

_____

_____

ABOUT THE AUTHOR

Kenneth Estrada is the lead pastor of Kingdom Life International Christian Center in Kissimmee, FL. *For over eighteen years, he has been loved by Lynette Estrada. Some would agree with her statements about him being her favorite person in the world because they see how well he loves her as Christ loves the Church. (Yes, this was inserted by Kenneth Estrada)* Together they have six beautiful children Therlisha, Isaac (Tico), Sandyna, Kezia, Ethan and Kenneth Mark (Cole).

Kenneth is a 2nd generation preacher and has been in ministry for over 20 years as a pastor and teacher. He is a 2003 graduate of RHEMA Bible Training College in Broken Arrow, OK. Known for his authenticity and his ability to deliver the Word of God mixed with humor, he has had the privilege of ministering in churches, conferences, and Bible schools in North America and abroad.

Through his preaching and teaching, you can see his heart for the Body of Christ to realize who they are in Christ, what they possess now in Him, and how to take their rightful place in Christ.

For more information visit us at
www.kennethestrada.com
www.wearekingdomlife.church

Kingdom Life AKA Estrada Ministries International
PO Box 580442, Kissimmee, FL 34758

Made in United States
Orlando, FL
08 May 2023

32927667R00104